DAVKA:

I

WILL

DANCE

By

NAOMI SILVER

Davka is a Yiddish word, one meaning of which is: "in spite of".

This book is a memoir, with all of the names and place-names changed to protect the not so innocent.

Davka is dedicated to all who long to dance.

WARM-UP

It is extremely foolish of me, but I wish I could be reincarnated as the zany flapper detective in *Miss Fisher's Murder Mysteries*, one of my favorite shows. Now that I have just passed my 81st birthday, Phryne Fisher is my ego ideal. Well, children dream of being Superman or Wonder Woman and no one blinks an eyelid in disapproval. To those cynics that claim this is a harbinger of my second childhood, I would say, "Everyone is entitled to their fantasies." Besides, my mother was once asked to spy on Nazi officers, while we were in hiding in Belgium, during World War Two. She was offered furs, gowns, jewelry. So maybe my scenario is not altogether farfetched. It would have made a great story, but she opted out. Of course, TV is better at providing happy endings. In real life, she might not have survived.

The clothes: one can only marvel at the clothes, especially the cloche hats, with maybe a stylish feather, or the fascinators, one more gorgeous than the other, gleaming on her perfectly groomed silky black hair. A half-hour's research online reveals that one can buy gold and silver head adornments at Etsy.com. Most of them seem too expensive and a mite too showy, even if my dance routine in one of our bi-annual Pro-Am showcases were to call for a Charleston. Also, I have to admit that, that no matter how glitzy, it wouldn't look as good on me, in my present incarnation.

Yes, I have been doing Ballroom Dancing for the last thirteen years and there have been choreographies that call for a flapper costume. However, it never comes close to measuring up to Miss Fisher's wardrobe.

Not only does she have great clothes, she has incredible moxie. She is the cleverest of detectives and wins over the dishy Inspector, who professes for many episodes to consider her a nuisance. When she climbs through a window in heels and a sassy skirt, to pursue important evidence, he wants to charge her for breaking and entering. He has his constable take mug shots for which she poses and mimes in the most charming way. Later one sees the Inspector smiling delightedly at the photographs. Of course, the charges are dropped. She has a luxurious motor car, flies her own airplane and saves many a situation, brandishing a small silver revolver.

I like the episode in which, at a stuffy soiree, she dances a torrid tango with a man, whose regular partner, his sister, has disappeared. It's the sort of tango in which the woman clenches a red rose, thorns and all, between her teeth. Was there a rose? I don't remember. Later she saves her partner, who of course has a somewhat unsavory reputation, from certain death. I haven't yet mastered the "torrid" in tango, though that too is part of my life, just without "the rose" or the ensuing dramas.

Besides her heroic acts, our super detective is also kind and adopts a delinquent girl, who is always in trouble at a snooty school, for, according to Miss Fisher, "doing the right thing." She often dances to affect some perilous rescue. In a later show there is a smooth waltz with the Inspector who is increasingly smitten with the resourceful and glamorous Lady Detective. Sometimes wishes do come true. But, alas, I will not be Miss Fisher—not in this lifetime. No one is in love with me these days, but I have fallen in love with dance and my life has taken a very unexpected turn this last decade.

1. PERILOUS TIMES

I was born at an odd time in history. Was there room for rejoicing? Times were perilous in the 1930s in Germany. The rate at which laws abrogating the rights of Jews to live in safety was about to explode exponentially. My physician father couldn't find work. My mother's previous unpleasant experience with an abortion, however, insured that I would live. There is one photo in which my father is holding me in his arms, looking lit up with delight. There are many other photos of a chubby baby and later of a solemn looking toddler with large brown eyes. I have only one memory of my early days. I see myself at age one and a half, just before we fled Germany, standing on a chair. My mother is adjusting the shoulder strap on a polka dot dress she made for me. I have never seen my mother sew or at least I never registered her in that role, but she told me that this really happened. There was a young woman, named Ruth, who was my nanny. I know her only from photos. I was told she was deported, along with the many relatives from my grandparents' immediate family, of whom I do not even have photographs.

When I was a teenager, my father made me a family tree, with crosses indicating which aunts and uncles and cousins were murdered by the Nazis. For many Jewish families, the birth of a child after the liberation meant a rebirth of hope, a cause for celebration. What about the birth of a child right as war was approaching, against the backdrop of Hitler's ravings? I know that my parents both loved me with immense tenderness, fraught with realistic fears for our survival, but.... My first language was German. It was dangerous to speak it out loud in Occupied Belgium. To protect all of us, my parents sent me, at the age of five, first to a convent, where I lived for a traumatic six weeks, and then to a Belgian family for the rest of the war. I learned French in Belgium, but I was neither German nor Belgian. For most of my life I have lived and dreamed in English. Am I American? I am an American citizen, but the feeling of not belonging anywhere persists, unsurprisingly, after such an inauspicious beginning.

2. DON'T RAIN ON MY PARADE

I am eight years old when I return to live with my parents after the war. My memory of that time is riddled with holes. It seems to me that no one talked to me about our three-year separation, about my stay in the convent, about my hiding parents, about the Nazis, about the war, about anything. Did anyone ask me about how I felt about being back "home?" I don't remember feeling anything. Nada. I ask my mother, as an adult, what I was like at that time. She said: "quiet. It was hard to re-connect." There are photos of me smiling. What does that mean?

This week I wake up from a dream in which some colleagues and I have organized a retreat for child survivors of trauma. I am talking earnestly to a young man, explaining that you have to re-experience your feelings, to emerge from numbness and go on with your life. Then I am with an eight-year-old girl and we are both crying. I wake up feeling unsettled. This week I have applied for restitution from the German Government, for persecution endured during the war. At my request, my daughter has sent me a copy of my father's German identity card. It has small swastikas and a big J for *Jude* on the front. My father seems so young in the small black and white photo. He couldn't have been more than 32 years old. I feel a pang: how frightened he must have been. How horrendous the ordeal was for this anxious man! He was scrupulous and particular. Here he is being hounded from place to place, finding refuge wherever he can, for however long he can. He and my mother stay for a while with a family that uses the pot in which they cook to wash their feet. My mother does everything in her power to keep that information from him. He would have starved. As it was, there is little enough to eat. He also ends up in a work camp in France, where they have to hang whatever bread is available out of reach of the rats. The train to the camp is bombed. There are many casualties. He is a doctor, but he has no way of treating anyone. Typhoid devastates the camp. There is nothing he can do. After a year or so, he escapes with false identity papers. Fortunately, the official on duty is distracted and doesn't look at his pass. The photo on the paper is that of an 18-year-old boy.

Today I was going to write about how "he rained on my parade" when I was a girl. I would be reading perhaps or doing something else innocuous. He would nag at me until I was in tears. This apparently happened frequently. A friend of the family validated the memory for me. Now that I think about it, in retrospect, it reminds me of the time when I was eight or nine when I hit a little girl for no apparent reason. What could he do with his feelings, after all? Yes, he was a grown-up. Yes, he should have known better, but perhaps it is time to forgive him. I do remember walking hand in hand with him after the liberation. He was telling me that it didn't matter about religion, that the main thing is to be a good person. That is my most vivid childhood memory of the two of us.

3. WHO I AM

I struggle up the stairs to the dance studio, holding on to the banister and leaning forward with my upper body. I have arthritic knees. I should have a partial knee replacement. I can't do that. It would mean not dancing for a few months.

Alexey, my teacher, greets me with, "How are you today?" He doesn't need to ask. He seems to know precisely how I am, perhaps through my body language. When he is free to start the lesson, he usually says: "Are you ready to be wonderful?" Hmmm…. First there is the warmup. If he judges, always correctly, that I am reasonably centered, it's the international style rhumba, to which there are a myriad of refinements. He may pick my favorite music, "Carnaval," from the movie *Black Orpheus*, for a smidgeon of extra motivation. He might begin to address some of the issues of technique, later in the lesson, if time allows. If I am obviously down or frazzled, we do my favorite, American tango. I have given him extra tango CDs. If I need to be woken up, he picks some upbeat electronic track from his own collection.

Then we get to my current routine, usually a choreography to be performed at the bi-annual Pro-Am showcase. I never miss it, at least so far, not even the time I have shoulder surgery and I am distraught. That time I had a piece from *Cabaret*: "Don't Tell Mama." I so didn't want to miss doing it, in my hot pink dance skirt that Natalya made for me, and the bustier that I borrowed from my daughter Genevieve. She told me her friends were mystified by her sending me a sexy piece of lingerie. As it turned out, the show was postponed, and I got to do my number! I love the naughty song: "Mama thinks I am in a convent, a secluded little convent in the South of France. She is not to know that I am dancing in a night club in a pair of lacy pants." I suppose that part of the fun is that I am in my seventies and that Sally Bowles, who tells everyone, "Don't tell Mama," is probably meant to be 18 years old.

What I discover, besides my passion for dance, is that *who I am* emerges in the dance. I am challenged to be more decisive, to be sure of myself (good luck with that!). As Alexey would put it, "You have to be on one foot or another. It doesn't work to be guessing and to be a little on each foot". He wants me to focus and to look at my partner. He says, "Not with one eye, with both eyes." Most troubling, is my tendency to go off into a trance state, to be off somewhere inside my head. Alexey will say: "What percentage of you is here today? 20 percent?" I might counter with, "No, it's 40 percent." He'll say: "Not bad for 20 percent. Imagine if 100 percent comes to the lesson!" Will that ever happen? I keep trying.

4. BARBARA

I remember my friend Barbara, in red leotards and tights, dancing a solo piece she had choreographed, called "The Jade Goddess." This was 62 years ago, when we were in college. She called herself Bunny at the time. She was slim and spry certainly, but after a while, "Barbara" seemed a more grown-up name. She considered "Barba," which I liked, but for most of our adult life it was "Barbara." Our friend James, a Black music major, at the almost entirely white and Jewish Brandeis University, had composed the music. For a long time, I could still hum the melody. James, with whom I studied and listened to music, both of us lying on my bed in the apartment I shared with Barbara, Junior Year, announced one day that we (he and I) were going to Japan after we got married. It had never occurred to me that he saw the connection between us as romantic. I liked listening to him talk about arcane subjects, such as John William Dunne (a British soldier, aeronautical engineer, and philosopher). Because I had no clue what this was all about, I thought he was brilliant and liked his company. Suffice it to say, when my father learned of my relationship with a Black man, he pulled me out of Brandeis, and I finished up college at CCNY. My father and I had already locked horns on this issue and I deeply resented his attitude. On the other hand, it turned out that my friend was psychotic. Also, I had been thrown into painful conflict by his insistence that we belonged together. I was shocked by his writing me, during my Summer in Israel, following this turbulent semester, that he would find me and follow me any place in the world. When he showed up at my door two years later, when I was already married, I was also somewhat spooked. On the other hand, he was the first person who ever made me feel special.

I wasn't dancing at that time, or not much anyway, so my contribution to "The Jade Goddess" performance was to do the spoken narration. I had, however, taken my first modern dance classes. This was at least a step beyond my dancing around the living room at home to "The Nutcracker Suite". The only radio station permitted at my parents' apartment in

Washington Heights, a heavily German Jewish neighborhood in those days, was WQXR, so I flitted around to the sound of classical music. At Brandeis, I was the recording secretary for the Modern Dance Club. Not very glamorous, I must say, but the group sponsored master classes by professional dancers, and I used to take the classes, hiding in the back. Barbara (Bunny) was the dancer. She had been paying, out of her pocket money, for her Graham technique classes all through High School.

We met sophomore year, wandering around the grounds of the college at night. She had some roommate problem and we talked for hours. Barbara tended to be dramatic and I liked being her confidante. Years later, she would call me at the apartment where I lived with my parents and would tell my perplexed father she needed to talk to me, because she was having a "trauma." In retrospect, after all these years, I know that Barbara talked me through more traumas than I can name on the spur of the moment. When we hit the fifty-year friendship mark, we decided to celebrate with a friends party. This idea came to Barbara as we were both dancing wildly to the intoxicating sound of drums at the Kripalu Institute on New Year's Eve. A large group of yogis in white robes had been solemnly chanting, "Om Nama Shivaya," over and over again for 24 hours. There was an air of expectancy. When, at close to midnight, the chanting gave way to drums, we cut loose, to dance in the new year. I remember someone jumping up and down and yelling "Shiva, Shiva." I was in a delirium of joy and moving hips with abandon. Someone shouted to me that I must have been a belly dancer in a previous life. Anyway, Barbara's idea bore fruit. We invited our closest friends to bring their best friend to the party. We laughed, we cried, we reminisced. My daughter, Julie, came and wrote an article about the event for *Lilith Magazine*. Her best friend didn't come, and she called her afterwards to tell her she had missed a hell of a party.

Barbara and I have danced together for so many years, at all kinds of events. We danced at the many birthday parties she threw for me since I was 18 years old. We danced at my daughter Julie's wedding. Julie was scandalized and complained that we looked as though we were stripping. Well, we weren't and isn't a wedding supposed to be a bacchanal? I think she was just worried that her new mother-in-law would disapprove. Nowadays, she would join us without hesitation. At my wedding, in the late 50s, Barbara was my maid of honor, but it was partner dancing and it was protocol to dance stiffly with my awkward young husband. Shall we have a party for the 60th anniversary of our friendship? I don't know. I do know that Barbara is coming to see me dance in my semi-annual dance showcase at the end of this month. I better remember to straighten my legs and point my toes.

5. ABOUT MARRIAGE

I am 22 years old. My parents warn me that I am going to be an old maid, like my aunt Ilse. My father tells me to wear lipstick and shorter skirts. I don't do make-up. I wear my brown hair in a long ponytail. I read a lot of 19th century writers. My favorite is Dostoevsky. I think that the question of whether I am marriageable material has been occupying my father's mind for some time. I think back to a family vacation. I am eighteen years old; I am reading Theodore Dreiser's *An American Tragedy* in back of the car. My father is driving with my mother in the passenger seat. I am close to tears towards the end of the book, when Clyde is arrested and they shave off his beautiful hair in prison, to prepare him for the electric chair. I think the part was played by Montgomery Clift in the movie version. You get the idea. At dinner, we have a perky waitress, who announces that she is going to college to get her "MRS" in the Fall. My father says to me: "Why can't you be more like her?" When my father finds me sobbing on my bed, he says, in his heavily accented English: "There's something wrong with you. You need a psychiatrist". Now, four years later, I of course, still don't have my Mrs. Above all, according to my father, I should stop spending my time with "that boy" and find someone I can marry. I consider "the boy,"

Martin, a close friend and tell him all my stories about real and imaginary boyfriends. Fifty years later, I understand that this is unforgivable cruelty. Once, my parents set me up with a respectable son of eminent parents, a lawyer or something of that sort. The trouble is that I like penniless poets and still do. On that occasion, my sometimes-mischievous mother hides the "boy," who happens to be visiting, in a back room of the apartment and barely restrains her laughter, as she sees me leaving for that totally forgettable date. One day, I am crossing Broadway at 156th Street, and I think about the love letters Martin has begun to send me. He writes me, "Take my hand. Let's be happy." I decide to marry him, on condition that he pays for my modern dance lessons. Can I be forgiven for my ignorance of the tenets of feminism? It is 1959 and we are both innocents. I might have said "yes" anyway because I am in love with his writing and it seals my fate. Years later, I am enthralled with his poems. My job is to hold the manuscript, while he performs at readings. Now, though, we are in love. We walk down the crowded streets in Washington Heights, our arms around each other, laughing at everything and everyone, including of course, my stuffy bourgeois parents. He is so full of joy, that I too feel that I can be lit up and be truly alive to everything around me. I am a survivor of war-torn Europe, of WWII. For now, history and family swept aside, I am joyous, hand in hand with an American. Martin talks fast, nonstop, jokes and puns, pouring out of him.

Sometimes I don't understand half of what he is saying and think he must be brilliant.

Our courtship has its unpromising moments. Once, at a party, he does an awkward cartwheel, totally out of context, just to show off. I say to myself, "Oh my God, I am marrying a jerk." I tell him that if he does this again, I am breaking up with him. Now, when I see him, long past divorce, at family weddings or Bar Mitzvahs, when he gets up on the empty dance floor, tipsy perhaps, bear-like, to do a clumsy dance, all by himself, I watch with amusement, without judgment.

At our big wedding, planned by my parents, I am 23 and he just turned 21. I find out years later that my parents had arranged for large plants to hide his family from the view of their more respectable guests. According to my parents, they had deplorable table manners. My prospective father-in-law, even, turned up for the families' first meeting not wearing a tie! My father is a German Jewish doctor and my mother comes from a wealthy German Jewish family, that, in the early 1900s, had servants and a chauffeur. My in-laws are working class. My tiny, blond mother-in-law is a lively Polish Jewish immigrant, who almost shouts when she speaks. My father-in-law, tall, dark and handsome, given to loud, brightly colored shirts and to a constant stream of jokes, had to quit college to support his mother and siblings during the Depression. He worked for a fruit store and so of course, did Martin. Horror of horrors, the family sometimes speak Yiddish! As to the young groom, to my father, he is still the "boy." He "is nothing and he has nothing!" When Martin asked my formidable father for "my hand in marriage," my father asked, how much money he made. When Martin said $4,000, my father queried, "a month?" "No," said my distraught, soon to be fiancé, "a year". Still, we are engaged (any husband is better than no husband at all) and my mother enjoys dressing him up in my father's tails. He looks classy, especially when he stands up straight. He has a tendency to slouch, which will increase with age.

He may be a writer, but a dancer he is not. My mother and I laugh for years, remembering our attempts to teach him to dance for the wedding. I understand that my father was the best waltzer in Berlin. What a come down! Martin, years later, writes a poem about our wedding night. He writes about our being "good little children," who carefully folded heavy towels on the hotel bed, so as not to soil the linen. After all these years, it still upsets me to think about the poem. He could have written that I was beautiful or sexy, or that he was in love, anything but the truth. Though I don't remember the wedding night at all, I am sure he is right. We know nothing about sex and all I know about passion is out of Dostoevsky and Flaubert. What I remember most is the relief that my parents could not come into the room and that I was free. My mother ends up liking him, though to her dismay, he has the habit of juggling her plates when we come for our bi-monthly, mandated visit. We, of course, also visit his parents. When we are still half a block away, I can hear my mother-in-law saying, "Here comes my handsome son." They are kind to me, but I could be Irma or Fanny, or any woman, for all that matters. I am their son's wife and am treated accordingly.

6. HOME

They say, "You can't go home again." I envy people who feel nostalgia for their childhood and for the place of their birth. In her book about emigrating, Eva Hoffman writes of her sadness as she sees the shore of her birthplace, Poland, receding.

I don't remember anything of Germany, the land which we had to leave to save our lives when I was one and a half years old. I see myself in photos, a chubby and cherished infant. There are also sepia photos of my grandparents, the women in elaborate gowns and extravagant hats. My favorite is of my beautiful mother, her eyes luminous staring into the future. She might be 23 years old and is wearing a white suit and a large, white, large-brimmed hat. Perhaps this is before the war, on her honeymoon in Italy.

I gather my parents paid a large sum during the war to someone who turned out to be a crook, for papers for South America. They changed their plan to flee to France when they were told that they most probably would be immediately arrested upon arrival. Belgium, a default choice, was soon occupied. We lived in a series of rooms, sometimes with other families. There are more stories and more photos, one of my parents and me, all of us looking somewhat disconsolate. It is unclear to me whether this photo was taken before or after the war. There is one of the three of us that I know was taken after the liberation. We are walking together, my father holding my hand and beaming into the camera.

Perhaps, not surprisingly, to me any place where I stay more than two days is "home," but there is no attachment, except perhaps to the house in which I have now lived 45 years. We lived in Belgium for nine years. I do remember our last apartment, to which I returned to be reunited with my parents after the war. There was a curtain separating my parents' bed from the rest of the room. I slept in a living room of sorts, perhaps on a couch. The toilet was down a flight of stairs and was used by several families. I remember clutching a reversible cloth elephant said to have come from America. We had a balcony overlooking the busy Avenue Rogier. There are photos of me smiling, also of my mother hugging me in the backyard of the building. I have pigtails and look happy enough. I don't remember parting from my parents when I went to live with a childless couple who had taken me in and had cared for me in their luxurious Villa. There were flagstones from which I pretended to dive into the water. But I do know that they told everyone I was their niece.

Could this have been a home, a comfortable house, apparently safe? There were even children, my first playmates. I learned to do cartwheels and handstands in the meadow. I played "house" with Raymonde, who lived next door, and with Jacques. Raymonde and I dug up earthworms to feed the family's hens. I remember tiny chicks in an incubator. There was a girl, named Jacqueline, who could walk on her hands. That impressed me greatly, but I never managed more than two steps before landing back on all fours. I lived there until the end of the war, but never looked back in longing, didn't even miss my "hiding parents". It seems rather strange. My parents told me to write to them afterwards, but I did so with reluctance, feeling I had nothing to say, no connections to that recent past in which they had played with me, hid Easter eggs for me, decorated the house for Christmas, made me dolls out of chestnuts and match sticks, gave me my first doll, with a hand-knitted dress and cap. There were also little magnetized dogs which fascinated me. I remember all of it, except for the parting. It's called psychic numbing, I think. I never looked back, though they saved my life and clearly loved me.

7. BEGINNERS' CLASS

My husband and I have a rocky start. Two days after our three-day honeymoon in the Catskills, Martin goes to report for his job, as a junior high school teacher. He sits for an hour in the office of the vice principal. When he finally enquires about what the next step is to be, the administrator tells him breezily, "Oh, Sorry, your job has been liquidated." Of course, it is my father who pays for my dance lessons, even though he says, "When are you going to stop taking those stupid lessons and take up tennis?" Still, he pays as he has also for college and for graduate school. Martin is an idealist. There has never been much money in that particular career track. He's a graduate of CCNY, where he is chided for reading lefty workers' papers in class instead of listening to the lecture. Later, when my younger daughter is a Brownie Scout, he protests that he doesn't want his daughter pledging allegiance, "under God." That's of course the end of the Brownies, for eight-year-old Genevieve, who likes the uniform.

At this juncture, he wants to "make knowledge viable to the young." This lofty aim loses some of its luster after his brutal initiation into teaching. The Board of Education posts him to an elementary school in the geographical center of Harlem. His fifth-grade class is handpicked. They are the most incorrigible kids in the school. When walking towards the school, the prostitute gives him the eye. He hears comments such as, "Eh, Man, you want to go?" He mutters politely, "No, thank you." He is after all, a well brought up Jewish boy, and until a few weeks ago, a virgin! He tells me of a ten-year-old girl, wearing green lipstick, who comes up to him in class and says, "You must be one of those Jewish niggers. Eat my pussy." On another day, a kid throws a bucket of red paint at the blackboard and it splatters on his new light grey suit. Another time, a few of his prize students hurl a volleyball right at his face. He is devastated when he loses his temper and wants to slap one of the children. He develops a series of illnesses and finally collapses, saying, "This is no job for a human being." During his 3-day absence from school, he is fired and replaced by the fifth teacher to attempt to deal with that special class for that semester.

Nevertheless, with some parental support, we have an apartment in Inwood, facing two synagogues. I feel like I have to look respectable when I leave the house. My long skirts are just fine. I take dance lessons at the New York Dance Center in Midtown Manhattan. Years later, I discover that it was originally a left-wing organization to overthrow the government by dance. I take the subway downtown once a week for a double class. I remember when the City had a blackout and my father picked me up by car and drove me home. He disapproved of my dancing, but there he was: "facta, non verba." I didn't register it at the time, but I would have wanted to be there every day. I am in Graduate School at Columbia doing a Master's degree in French Literature, somewhat grandly called "Romance Philology and French". I don't think I am smart enough to take a degree in Comparative Literature, my college major. But I am fluent in

French, so assume that I have a leg up. At the Dance Studio, I take Graham technique, Humphrey Weidman, Lester Horton, Haitian-Caribbean, and one Jazz class. My favorite is Lester Horton with its long, clean lines. I go to Advanced Beginners' class and, with trepidation, because I fear I am not good enough, take the occasional Intermediate class. One of my much-liked teachers, long, tall Joyce Trissler, yells at me, "Straighten your legs. They look like spaghetti." To this day, I remember the day that Donald McKayle takes my hand and leads me in a step that eludes me. The students have to dance across the floor in a diagonal line. I avoid being first or last, preferring to hide in the middle. It doesn't appear that I am ready to perform before an audience. I am discouraged by my slow progress. But I loved it and don't understand today what triggered my quitting shortly after my younger daughter Genevieve's birth in 1965. It's all unclear. I am sure I didn't dance during my pregnancies. I had passed the defense of my Master's Thesis, shortly before the birth of my older daughter Julie in 1962. There was no way I could have failed. The three professors interrogating me were terrified that I was going to give birth right in the office.

It seems that I didn't dance for years after leaving the N.Y. Dance Center. but I remember that even before Genevieve was conceived, when Martin and I went to a staff party at Commerce H.S. where he taught, I got pulled on to the dance floor by a 6'2" skinny Black man. His dance consisted mostly of his nodding his head vigorously to the rhythm of rock and roll music, popular at that time. I was thrilled, doing my own thing, free style. After that there were regular dance parties with other teachers. They came to our new, larger apartment in Queens, scandalizing the neighbors with the music and also because our friends were mostly Black. I remember that one of them, Cliff, committed suicide, or maybe it was a drug overdose. I knew nothing. No one shared any details. I was sad because I particularly liked Cliff. I understood nothing except the rhythm of the music and the joy of moving my body. Perhaps there is a theme emerging for me. Pina Bausch said, "Dance, dance or we are lost." I don't know about her saying until 50 years later, but I remember thinking, while dancing at a party, that this was the way to affirm life, to defeat the fear of death, that in times of plague, people must have, should have danced.

8. MOTHER LORE

She's standing on the *Rue de la Paix* in wartime. She's wearing the Yellow Star branding her as a Jew. She is 28 years old, living wherever she can with her severe doctor husband and her three-year old daughter. It is dangerous to be discovered covering up the Star. Occasionally she does hide it for a moment and is amused to see the German soldiers flirt with her and to witness their consternation when they realize that she is just a dirty Jew. She takes chances. She refuses to go down into the bomb shelters when the V1s come pounding out of the sky.

The luxurious honeymoon in Italy took place in a different life. She loved the fine hotels, her silk dresses, her stylish hats. But she waited in vain for her bridegroom to tell her she was beautiful. She will remember that he failed to dance with her at their wedding and fell asleep on their wedding night, overcome with too many unaccustomed alcoholic drinks. She can only guess at the mysteries of sexual passion. She has read romances, seen movies, gossiped with her girlfriends.

None of this matters anymore during the war. She misses her parents, who have fled to Palestine. After the War, they will send large crates of oranges, but that is years in the future. For now, day by day, the task is not to be arrested by the Gestapo, to find shelter and food. She and the child live with her parents-in-law while her husband is interned in Gurs, in France, as a German enemy alien. She sees him off at the train that is to take him to the Camp. She carries a suitcase with some warm blankets and raw eggs (there wasn't time to cook them). She is a beautiful woman and the man guarding the prisoners turns his back so she can heave the suitcase through the window of the train, silently sanctioning her act. Her husband is away for a year and escapes the camp just before it falls under the governance of the Nazis.

She likes to remember that in the midst of the darkness she and her sister-in-law would often go to a *café dansant*, dancing with whomever asked, including German officers. She wasn't wearing her Star on these outings. Was this before the edict? It seems unlikely and it was imprudent perhaps, but they wanted so much to be young and to live. On one of these outings, she is approached by two men. They are most probably the Belgian Resistance, she thinks. They ask her to join a network of spies. The organization would provide her with gowns, furs, jewelry. A woman like you could infiltrate the higher echelons of the Nazi hierarchy, they tell her. She promises to think about it and to meet them at the same café the following week. But this road she does not take. It might have made a moody black and white film, but it was likely to end with torture and death.

As it is, her days are far from glamorous. The child is wakeful and cranky, keeps asking for her father. She, at a loss to explain, says he has gone to the butcher, the baker, the tailor, whatever comes to mind except for the impossible truth. She is the one to carry the coal for the stove up several flights of stairs in the Winter. Food continues to be scarce. They share kitchens and toilets with other families. The hygiene isn't always up to par and when her husband returns from the camp, she does her best to hide this from him, who though already starved would never have eaten another morsel had he known. She is the one to go out on the street to trade their ration coupons for small amounts of food. The diet consists mostly of turnips and potatoes and sometimes a little bread. Once she steals a potato from a vegetable stand. Sometimes she walks her brown-eyed three-year old daughter to a bakery and coaches her to ask for a small loaf of bread. They are Belgians. Jew-hating or not, no one refuses the child, though Nazis we now know were capable of dashing babies' brains out against a granite wall in front of their parents. We also know, now, about the families ordered to undress after the harrowing trip in cattle cars, to then be herded to the gas chambers and their death. Their clothes and belongings are left behind to be sorted by the Nazis, who take whatever is valuable and burn the rest.

What does she suspect? She may know that deportation probably means death. Too many times she, her husband, and her daughter flee from one no longer safe hiding place to another temporary room. One day, a Belgian SS man approaches her and proposes she move in with him. He will throw out the other woman, the one who currently enjoys his hospitality. She can have food, silk stockings, whatever she wants. Week after week, she finds reasons to put him off. She reminds him how dangerous it would be for him to cohabit with a Jewess, that he risks prison or worse. He is undeterred, so the time comes when it is imperative to move on. Her husband has found a place for himself and the child, where she is to join them. As she comes down the stairs with her belongings, he suddenly appears. He asks if she is moving because of him and adds, "My people can find you anywhere." Without missing a beat, she answers, "That's good. Then I don't have to give you my address."

The family survived and is re-united after the War and, in 1948, after a 15-day trip on the New Amsterdam, they land in Hoboken, New Jersey. They have gotten an affidavit from an American politician and are to live, briefly, in London Terrace in New York City. She tells her daughter, many years later, that they sat on their suitcases for three hours after landing, waiting for someone to pick them up. After all the years of hiding from the Gestapo, the bombs, the hunger, the uncertainty about who was going to survive, she felt safe, just waiting for what was to come next.

9. INFIDELITIES

In time, life and work keep improving. My husband, Martin, and I have two daughters. He is a professor and a poet. I am a clinical social worker. We own a house in the suburbs. That is all predictable. But, fifteen years into the marriage, he is falling in love with other women, with increasing frequency. The light in his blue-green eyes has gone out. His eyes look empty. He needs a new romance to bring him to life. He is given to confessing and asking me for absolution. There is the six-month affair, which he makes some effort to camouflage. I am in despair and imagine the woman is lovely and lyrical. She turns out to be a hard-faced alcoholic who is known to be abrasive and difficult at the college where they both teach. I don't know whether to be relieved or disappointed. He has a brief flirtation with a student and proposes to meet with her jealous husband, to proclaim her innocence. I try to dissuade him, telling him that he is likely to get beaten up. The outcome is that the husband smashes a custard pie into Martin's face.

One Summer day, it's different. He is *really* in love, with a woman who is leaving her husband and four small children to be with him. He tells me that he might have to be with the woman of his dreams, that he is planning to leave me. I throw my wedding ring into the bushes, down a hill. He retrieves it, but nothing has changed. That we are both almost 50 years old and have been together 25 years, makes no difference. Mind you, he doesn't move out until I kick him in the shins and throw a lamp at him. My mother-in-law says, "Good for you. You're not his therapist!" I wake up the next morning and say to myself, "Oh my God. I am all alone." My parents agonize over who is going to pay the bills, until I ask them to stop and tell them they are not helping me.

10. THE BLUE ORGANDY DRESS

They used to have an expression: "you're ugly and your mother dresses you funny." At eleven-years old, new to the U.S. from Europe, I wasn't precisely ugly, but I did "dress funny." I remember a red print dress, with a heart-shaped bodice that was too tight on my chubby body. More precisely, I remember the photograph of me in pigtails, looking to one side and down at the ground, away from the camera, as I always did. I arrived in New York City in time for fifth grade. I learned English so quickly that I don't remember the process. The teacher liked me, no doubt because I was super polite. My classmates kept their distance. I read in a slam book that some of them considered me "stuck up." One day, for some reason, my mother (let's blame her, why not?) dressed me in a light-blue organdy party dress. During recess, having nothing else to do, I went for a walk in the park across the street from the school. I was alone, of course. Who would be seen with this odd-ball immigrant in a blue organdy dress? A group of girls gathered around me, snickering and pointing at my dress. Before I knew it, I had hauled off and smacked the girl standing nearest me, hard in the face. I don't know if anyone was more surprised than I was.

In any case, the dressing "funny" continued to be a problem in Junior High School, or so it seemed to me. My parents insisted I carry my books in a briefcase. What a ridiculous idea. I hated that bag. All the other girls carried their books in their arms, elegantly stooped over their burden. Also, I had to wear ugly beige tights in the winter. Eventually I wore bobby socks, like everyone else, that kept sliding into my loafers. I don't know if my classmates had to stop every block or so, too, to pull up their socks. By my senior year, amazingly, I was part of a group of four girls who met weekly at one of their apartments. At fourteen, we thought of ourselves as an "anti-boys club." How cool was that?! We would spend an hour or so, acting out parts of a Shakespeare play. I remember standing on a chair, reciting, "Romeo, Romeo, wherefore art thou Romeo?" Is that why I am still looking for people who will join me in reading Shakespeare aloud? I had more luck in Junior High School.

Then we had a prom to go to. I had a purple hand-me-down dress, which I liked. It made me look thinner. It was Lenore, Margery, Rhoda, and me. We went together and none of us got to dance, not even once. When someone now asks me whether I danced as a girl, I can truthfully report that I was a "wallflower." That means I got to help prop up the walls. When we left the dance, the other girls were downcast. I think it was Lenore who said: "We are social flops." I, on the other hand, was happy. I belonged, even if it was to a group of "social flops."

11. AUGUST, 1986

On an August morning, with the sun unforgiving, my 23-year-old daughter Julie and I get into my dented green Toyota and set out over the George Washington Bridge, to meet friends at a Delaware beach resort. I am warily scanning the lanes, crowded with cars honking and jockeying for position, hoping to choose the right one, the one noted in my written directions. Three hours into the trip, my uncertainty mounts. Have we taken the right road? I get lost everywhere. I am especially lost right now. Map reading is out of my comfort zone and you can't ask directions on the highway. Then we spot a sign, saying, "Delaware Water Gap." It's not on the directions, but we must be on the right track. I pay the toll and drive on to the bridge. We don't say much. My thighs stick to the seat of the car and I stare into the long road ahead, looking for signs that tell me we're on our way, finally. Four hours later, we arrive at Rehoboth. We are sodden with fatigue and grief. Our friends embrace us with solicitude and relief that we have arrived.

Martin left me in July, two days after my 49th birthday, having decided to be together with his new love. My daughter is as shocked as I am. Last year at our 25th anniversary celebration, she toasted us as "the only happily married couple I know."

The sun is already setting. We walk down to the beach. All is calm on the horizon. I feel the warm water lapping over my toes. There is a full moon. My husband and I have embraced every experience together for half a lifetime. This moment, this memory is mine alone.

12. THE OTHER WOMAN'S HUSBAND

One day I get a call from this guy, who says he's married to Myrna. Myrna is the new love of my husband's life. I agree to meet this man under the clock at Grand Central Station, Tuesday at noon, high noon perhaps. Do we face off, commit double Hari Kari, fall into each other's arms? I wonder what he's like.

Martin and I had been married 25 years. The last time he was in love, I played the vamp for a while. When that didn't work, I found myself staring into space, not able to say much, or not wanting to. In any case, that great love didn't last, and I hoped Myrna, too, would go away. But it was different this time. "He had to leave," he said.

I got ready to meet the betrayed husband. I put on an emerald green silk blouse. The color suits me. Walter, the husband, turns out to be slight and pale. He tells me that he has lost 20 lbs. in the last month, hence the melancholy poet look. Alas, I have only lost 15 lbs. by this time. We look at each other and I imagine him thinking that I am no match for Myrna. Indeed, he proceeds, in his mournful way, to tell me so as we order our tea. He has regular Lipton. I choose chamomile. Neither one of us is hungry for anything less than solace. He tells me that Myrna has extraordinary talents in bed, can and will do anything. They haven't however had sex in five years. "He must be a wonderful lover," says Walter, wistfully. She's wanton and romantically thin. She has four little children, whom she is prepared to abandon for my irresistible husband. The children are aged four, six, nine, and eleven. She has always been a wonderful mother. I feel utterly routed by this flaming siren. Martin has complained that he and I are too much like brother and sister, that there isn't enough passion between us. Walter keeps talking. He tells me that she has bought sexy new clothes. On their birthday she ran out on her children and the birthday cake ritual to be with her lover. She left a steaming love letter right on her bed. I change the subject. I don't need the details. I try to console him; tell him she'll be back. He hints he'll have his rival followed and roughed up. This does not bode well for our becoming a swinging foursome. Mainly I harbor fantasies of beating in sexy Myrna's face. I am told by friends, who have seen her, that she's nothing to look at. She has glasses and is flat chested. "He must be mad," they say. Well, what can friends say under the circumstances? Decidedly, we are not going to be friends. I am not too keen on Walter either at this point. I am not up to the task of giving him sympathy. He had better pay for his own tea, as well. I don't want to hear further tales of Myrna's sexual prowess. I do not want to think of Walter trying to explain to four small children that Mommy is off on an adventure. Most of all, I don't want to imagine the adventure.

This is all ancient history now. Martin now lives, happily, I presume, with his younger third wife and has retired, after years as a tenured full professor at a City University. He is now training to be a psychoanalyst. Even the trauma of our separation seems long past and almost forgotten. But at the time, my grief is violent. I scream in my car driving home from work or from my yoga class, but I never miss a day of work. Then, I go on with my life.

But it isn't until 2003 that I take formal dance lessons again. Sorry, Dad, just as you predicted, I don't make any money either from my degree in Romance Philology and French or with my dance. On the other hand, in spite of your disapproval, it is your foresight in leaving me some money that makes it possible for me to pay for this dance obsession. I am told you were an excellent dancer. Would you, in some part of you agree that, "You walk with your feet, but you dance with your heart?"

13. NEXT DANCE

The day after Thanksgiving, Martin tells me he wants a legal separation. The following day, my daughter Genevieve and I have plans to go dancing at Shea's Barefoot Ballroom. I don't know how she finds these places, but I am game. First, we meet for dinner at Marianne's, a Mexican Restaurant on 21st Street and Eighth Avenue. Yes, I am crying hysterically before driving downtown. My other daughter, Julie, who lives with me at the time, begs me to call my therapist. She keeps trying to call her father to yell at him. I keep grabbing the receiver from her hand to hang up and she finally gives up. By the time I am seated at the restaurant, I have calmed down. We are discussing that joke in *Annie Hall* about adult education being such a wonderful thing, and, despite or because of the fact that my husband ran off with his adult student, we find the concept so funny that we can't stop laughing. With a few sips of Genevieve's margarita, I am slightly tipsy. We are laughing as I pass the second part of my drink across the table. We notice a gentleman, sitting down at a little table, just a foot away from where we are having our uproarious party. Genevieve, never shy, says hi. While I go to the ladies' room, the two of them have arranged for us to go to coffee after dinner. Our new friend, Paul, is distinguished looking. Genevieve later declares him "dashing" and I give him my phone number.

After coffee, Paul excuses himself and Genevieve and I go dancing. The only rules at Shea's are "no shoes, no smoking, no alcohol." It has a beautiful wooden floor and dance studio mirrors. Most of the dancers are in their twenties with a smattering of older people like me, in all kinds of outfits. I don't remember what I was wearing, but remember Genevieve's having a long scarf, and doing a flowing dance, à la Isadora Duncan. At the end of the evening an earnest young man asks my permission to marry her. Some people dance in couples or in groups of four or five. One man practices his ballet positions in front of the mirror. The music is mostly rock or disco, with interludes of mellow electronic music more suited to the ballet dancers in the group.

A week later, to escape my utter desolation about my husband's moves to finalize the separation, I take myself to the 92nd street Y for a folk dancing class. I know nothing about folk dancing and find it more complicated than I had anticipated. Another woman and I team up and do our own version of the dance. The instructor scolds us. We are not completely cowed but proceed to behave ourselves like good little children and make an effort to learn the steps. I find out that dancers tend to be serious about their discipline, be it folk dancing, square dancing or ballroom. Neophytes' creativity is not necessarily appreciated. Well, it was nevertheless fun at the time.

On my first date with Paul (because he did call, as promised), we have a tense dinner at a Thai Restaurant. Afterwards, we go dancing at Sounds of Brazil, otherwise known as SOB's. Although he dances well, and in spite of the lively Latin music, I am not enamored of him. He is much older than Martin and is grumpy over dinner. It will take time until we get a groove on.

We date, we talk on the phone, we do museums, films, walks in Riverside Park. It isn't until four months later, when I see my ex at a friend's funeral and decide I don't like him, that I am "in," beginning to be in love, if you will. I drive down to Chelsea, where he lives, twice a week and it all feels like a *Roman Holiday*. We have cannolis and cappuccino on Second Avenue. I stay overnight. We make love, sometimes on a futon in front of his fireplace. He says, "When I first met you, I felt I had known you my entire life. Then brute reality set in." He has a slight English accent, having lived in Spain and in England for many years. We discuss books. He gives me two novels to read and for my comment. This is probably a test, but I love both of his choices. He says with surprise, "You understand what I am talking about. Usually no one does." Eventually, he asks me to go away on a weekend with him and I hear myself saying, "Yes." I wonder if I need to keep this a secret. My children already know about my two visits to Chelsea every week. They are not the least bit shocked. I am happy!

Two years later, my ex gets married again. It will be the second of his third marriages. Now, twenty-nine years later, from the perspective of an obsessed dancer, I ask myself, "How does he do it? He can't even dance." I won't mention any other issues, but the series of marriages does give rise to a number of awkward family occasions, when all three wives are present.

Eventually Paul moves in with me and we create a life for ourselves. He is my love for the next fifteen years. But then a shadow falls over our lives when he is diagnosed with cancer. On my 64th birthday, my friend Barbara has a birthday party for me. Paul and I dance our last dance together to the Nina Simone version of, "Ne me quitte pas." His legs are swollen with lymphedema. We move slowly, holding on to each other. Two months later we are scattering his ashes in the Hudson River, Barbara, Julie, his son Ben, and myself.

14. SITTING IN THE SUN

I remember sitting in Riverside Park, on the granite steps, leaning into Paul, early Spring. There's still a nip in the air, early April with the pale sun on our faces. We are happy. Paul loved the sun. On vacations, he wanted to lie on the beach, take in the sun. I was pulling in the other direction, wanting to go hiking, horseback riding, do whatever activity was on offer. Once I talked him into going horseback riding in the breathtaking mountains in Costa Rica. It was just the two of us and a boy guide. We were ambling along, taking in the sights, when the guide mischievously cracked the horses with a whip. All of a sudden, we were cantering, like mad, me shrieking with delight, Paul quiet, but perhaps, not quite as enthusiastic.

How often did we sit and savor Spring and Fall, so jubilant with color and even the bare branches in Winter? In the last few years of Paul's life, there was cancer, the silent intruder. We would sit on the deck and I would bring out slices of peach and mango, strong coffee. He might be starting chemo or having major surgery the next day. He would say, "I don't want to talk about it" and would sip his coffee and taste the sweet fruit. In Spain, where we visited his son a month before he died, he would order a cortado, an espresso in a small cup, at an outdoor cafe. It was never a large amount of anything. He liked tasting life, in all its varieties. Here in New York City, sitting in cafés in the Village or in Alphabet City, he would say, "Let's watch the world go by." He was a writer and looked and listened. He would nod towards a group of people and would ask me, "How do you think those people are related to one another?" He had a good ear for dialogue. He, himself, didn't talk that much and was slow to tell me of his adventures. Once, early in our relationship, as we were walking around a lake, he said to me, "You don't always have to build conversational bridges." "Oh," I thought, "It's okay to just be together, you don't have to work so hard to connect."

When he was dying, in the ICU, at Montefiore Hospital, he couldn't talk because of a tracheotomy tube. He wrote me a note, "I can't talk. Just sit by me. If I need something, I will write."

15. FIREBIRD

In the last year of Paul's life, my friend Barbara got tickets for all of us for a performance of the ballet *Firebird*. We made our way slowly across the quadrangle at Lincoln Center under the blazing July sun. Paul soldiered on without complaint, as was his way. It was meant to be a birthday treat for his September birthday. We didn't know it, but he was to die at the end of August after his fourth major surgery for bladder cancer.

After the surgery, the surgeon advised that his son should fly in from Spain immediately. Paul was in and out of reality in those weeks. He would say to his son, Ben, "Let's go out to lunch, we can come back afterwards," or "Let's go to the movies tonight." It was clear, of course, that he was dying. I had to run out of the room. One day, he knew, and said, "I am finished. I am not going anywhere anymore." Sometimes, he hallucinated that he was back on the houseboat in Paris, where he met his wife, fifty years ago. On what was to be his last day, Ben and I visited with him for a while, though he was unconscious. We took breaks wandering around the bustling Bronx. On the way home I found myself sobbing. I had to go back. I asked Barbara to drive back with me. We sat with him for an hour. He probably was not aware of our presence, but I felt better. Early the next morning, the call came. He had died at five a.m. We rushed over to see him one more time. I kissed his forehead and his swollen hands. I cried.

But he had experienced *Firebird*. It was an inspired gift to a man who loved Stravinsky. It was pure magic. Everything ceased to exist in that moment except for the dance with its vibrancy. We were mesmerized. It was fire, it was life.

16. BALLROOM

I am 68-years old when I start taking ballroom dance lessons with tall Al. I had cut out a clipping in the local paper about the school about three years before and tacked it on my bulletin board. Every once in a while, I looked at the photo of teacher and student and every once in a while, I said to myself, "It's too expensive, I'm sure. I can't afford it."

I meet Al at an Inter-Village swing class and we partner up and pal around sometimes. Al is a character. He has the habit of telling people that I would be perfect, if only I were a blonde. I am a very petite brunette and don't intend to do anything about my hair color, except to get it colored brown, every six weeks or so. One day, I meet him in front of the Library and blurt out, "What do you think of taking dance lessons together and sharing the cost?" He says, "Break my arm," and offers to pay for all of it. Clearly, he is enthusiastic, but I will pay my share. We take private lessons with Alexey. It turns out that hc and his wife Natalya were world champions in Russia. He is charming and encouraging in spite of our labored slow progress learning the basic salsa step. The first time Al and I go to one of the dance socials, I am in awe. There are strobe lights in the studio and women in filmy clothes dance to rhythmic and sensuous music. It all looks exotic, impossible to learn. I will never be one of those graceful women. Al doesn't seem to be nervous, but he can't dance unless he first consults his notes.

Eventually I opt for private lessons with Alexey, and never mind the cost. It's a brand-new world. In spite of my worries about hurting Al's feelings, he accepts my wanting to move on without him with good grace. Alexey says, "This is not a walk in the park like with Al," and I get a little closer to being able to dance at a social if someone asks me.

I am the oldest student at the studio, except for Joan, who is in her eighties. She competes and wins prizes. At one of the showcases, I remember her spinning and her skirt unfurling, revealing a more daring costume underneath. She can't walk very well, but against all odds, she dances. A few years later, I find myself in a similar situation. So many of my joints are arthritic that I no longer go to the orthopedist, as I can't decide where I most urgently need a cortisone shot. My wardrobe changes. Alexey wants me to wear colors and skirts and dresses that flow. He says my Eileen Fisher skirts are elegant, but not suitable for dancing. Also, he requires dance shoes with heels. One of the students, Mia, who does competition, tells me about Worldtone, a dance shoe store in Manhattan, and I make my way there to buy shiny open-toed dance shoes with tiny crystals on the straps.

I do my first dance showcase with Bill. He's a lovely, dark complexioned, svelte young man with hypnotic brown eyes. We rehearse an international rumba routine. Alexey tells me (no doubts thinking of my staid wardrobe), that costumes are of great importance to the show. On his recommendation, I rent Mia's sparkling, lavender ball dress. I have never worn anything this marvelous in my life. Years later, I reflect that the dress being floor length hides my footwork, which is, unsurprisingly, not up to par. I am flexible and do the "lines" well, that is the showy stuff. I am not nervous. I imagine it doesn't matter what I do. The dress will carry the night. My new friend, Amanda, takes half an hour to do my makeup. I fear I look somewhat like a superannuated hooker. Everyone reassures me that you need a lot of blush, mascara, eyeliner, and very red lipstick to look good under the lights. About forty students are performing with either Alexey, his wife Natalya, or with Bill. The venue has a huge ballroom with chandeliers. There's dinner and the show for around 125 guests. Natalya and Alexey perform several breathtaking numbers. All of it is very expensive, but it is irresistible. Alexey says, "For one night you get to feel what it's like to be a professional dancer." For the following nine years I will prepare to do two showcases a year.

The venue may be less glamorous these days, and there's a dwindling audience, but it is still special, and I continue to long for my friends and family to come see me dance. That night I have an admiring audience, my daughter Julie and my friends Barbara, Debby and Amanda. Later, I hear Julie telling her husband on the phone, "My mother was amazing!" I am a star! That illusion gets dispelled quickly, as I get more deeply into my dance obsession.

Amanda wants me to go dancing with her and she won't take "no" or "maybe" for an answer. We go to Westchester Ballroom, where I sit for two hours and nobody asks me to dance. I want to cry. It's humiliating. Also, it is painful to hear music and not be able to dance. Amanda tells me I have to ask the men. I don't dare unless they look crippled or hopelessly unattractive. We hear a lot about Jude's Dance Center. We find our way there. Amanda wants me to call her when I leave my house and then if I get there before she does. For good measure she wants me to call her when I get home at night. Half concerned, mostly joking, I think, she says, "Oh my God, Naomi. You're blind. Call me when you get home." She teases me about doing a cha cha with a white cane. No matter how offensive she gets, I find myself laughing like a loon. It is true I have poor night vision and absolutely no sense of direction. Sometimes I drive up to Chappaqua, where she lives, so we can go to the social together. On my third attempt, I find my way to her house without her having to come rescue me out of some cul de sac. Her little dog, Doobie, barks wildly when I arrive. She shares a parking lot with another house, and it takes me a while to maneuver in and out without crashing into another car. Amanda looks me over, comments on my outfit, tells me I need more blush and adjusts whatever needs adjusting on my dress. On snowy nights, when I balk at going out, she admonishes me on the phone, "How many Friday nights are you going to have to go dancing?" I give in, put on my finery and my glitzy jewelry and pack my shoes and drive into whatever weather, to the destination for that night.

I heard someone say that the longer you dance, the shorter the skirts and the longer the earrings you find yourself wearing. There's some truth to that. Besides Jude's Dance Center we go to Connecticut to "Let's Dance Tonight". This venue is in a mansion, the dance in a huge hall, reminiscent of an oversized Junior High School gym. Amanda is 15 years younger than I and gets asked to dance more often than I, by better dancers, and I am jealous. One night we can't find a dance. We drive around in her car, with the music blaring. We drive around for hours, laughing and singing. Amanda won't give up. Here we are, Thelma and Louise, without the tragic ending. Not only are we going to live, but we are going to find a dance, well maybe not that night, but there is always next weekend!

17. THE PARADISE DANCE ACADEMY

A dancer at the studio is changing into street clothes when I arrive. I am already wearing my over-the-knee, flair, black dance skirt. To be ready for my lesson, I just have to put on my thick-heeled, well-worn practice shoes. Emil, my tango teacher, complains that these are men's shoes. Alexey says they are warrior's shoes, battered and bloody from use. Alright, so I can't wear sexy stiletto heels, the typical tango shoes. Most dance shoes hurt my feet. At milongas, whenever I am sitting out a dance, I glance longingly at the women's pretty shoes.

The lovely blonde dancer might be 17-years old. She is wearing flesh colored Capezio fishnet tights and three-inch satin shoes. Her mid-thigh black skirt hugs her slender hips. I have seen her dancing. Every movement is sharp and precise.

In the antechamber students and teachers are milling about waiting for their lessons, stretching, chatting and even dozing. Some are perched on stools around an elevated high table eating yogurt or evil-tasting healthy shakes, probably kale mixed with banana. I overhear a young brunette in tights and leotards, yelling into her cell phone: "Ma," she says, "Don't worry, I will get a job." I wonder about the mother of the woman on the phone. Maybe she's tired of supporting her artistic children. Maybe the daughter is planning to go to L.A. with her rocker boyfriend. No, that's too cliché. All the action is in New York anyway, or is it Chicago? Or is Viet Nam the cool place to go nowadays? In any case, she can't take a break from her dance training. That would be fatal, I think

I am a plodding, ancient being, envious of these talented, apparently self-assured youngsters. I am hesitant when I move. It's a personality trait that manifests itself on the dance floor, just as it does everywhere else in my life. I need to work against this tendency, especially in the Latin dances. Even now, I learn so much about myself as I continue to take dance lessons.

But I'm old and therefore I'm invisible. Nevertheless, a young man in black practice shoes addresses me. He asks if I take my lessons at Fred Astaire. I answer no, that my teachers are Alexey and Natalya Kirsanov. His face lights up and he says, "They were famous in Russia. We used to watch them. We looked up to them. They were champions. My God, they are dinosaurs now." I bask in reflected glory, but think that my teachers, vital and under forty, are hardly extinct.

Natalya, a petite blonde, smiles when I tell her of my encounter. Of course, I leave out the "dinosaur" part. She says that those were exciting times and she misses those years when she and Alexey competed and often won. Even now, when Natalya dances, even if she is only teaching, it is nearly impossible to watch anyone else. When I tell the story to Alexey, he says that this was a different life. He is happy in the present with his two red-headed children, his teaching, designing homes and collaborating with builders. Last month, he hauled a ton of cement and hurt his back. He doesn't complain and I hear this from Natalya. I tell him, "What are you doing, Alexey? You are the brains of the building operation. You shouldn't be doing heavy manual labor. Remember you have to dance and do lifts with your students." I am certainly not the first person to give him this advice, but, of course, Alexey will do as he pleases. He arches his eyebrows and marvels at his two-year old daughter's stubbornness, laughing and saying, "Where does she get it from?"

When I tell him about the virtuosity of the dancers at Paradise Ballroom, he says, "But they do what I teach you, right?" I think, yes, but they are professionals, they are electric, they are young. Sometimes, I look at their unlined faces and their shapely, muscular bodies, and I think of all the challenges that lie ahead for them, especially as dancers: career, love, children, maybe injuries and illness, good luck and bad. I have cleared so many hurdles in my almost 80 years of life. I wonder at my bleak outlook. Why not think of the joys, of the epiphanies to come?

I heard somewhere that old people are happier, they can be more content in the moment, don't have to struggle so much. I am happier, but only because these last ten years I am finally dancing. Is this my envy speaking? Am I saying,

"You will be old someday too"? It's not so bad being old, but still, I keep hearing in my mind, "They are not long, the days of wine and roses." Ah yes, but the wine is intoxicating. The scent of roses lingers. I am old, but I still want to dance, to laugh, to love.

18. SHOWTIME

It is one week from the bi-annual pro-am showcase. It sounds rather grand when you say it that way, but as we get closer the students get gloomier, look more worried.

In the previous months, I have hunted in the stores and on the internet for pieces of my costumes. For the drum piece, I now have a lilac leotard to go with the purple jumpsuit, and the quest for a belt and necklace have led me to Bellydance.com and success. The t-shirt for the rap number is another matter. Alexey laughs as he tells everyone how much I love the music, a vulgar and silly song by Pit Bull. I find there are shirts with the picture of a pit bull and that some of the more vivid ones cost up to $200. Julie brings me my grandson Adam's jeans, torn at the knee. My foot gets stuck in the hole, when I try to put them on. The shirt is supposed to be eye catching, glitzy and "street." In the end, with my friend Samuel's help, I decorate a black shirt with "NS 666" on the back and a cartoon picture of lightning on the front. I paste little gold sequins for the image, but they keep falling off.

My t-shirt is still shedding, and I am talking to myself at five a.m., asking myself, "How could you spend so much money, having lessons almost every day for the last six months? It boggles the imagination. Probably the performances won't be much good anyway. This has to stop." Promising that I will practice fiscal austerity from now on doesn't really calm me enough to allow me to drift off to sleep. I try to relax by going through my various routines, remembering Alexey's admonitions. For example: "Have the elbow higher than the hand; on the hip thrust, keep your eyes on the mirror (on the audience, at the show); don't take extra steps; don't miss any steps; hands and feet should be active; relax but focus. So, why doesn't any of this help me sleep?

I get out of bed, take some Tylenol, consider half a Xanax, toast myself half of a sprouted grain muffin and eat it with soy cream cheese, write in my journal, get back into bed, again close my eyes. I must have fallen asleep because my alarm clock wakes me at nine a.m., in time for my lesson and my discussion with Alexey about my new plan. Alexey says that I sound like an alcoholic, hoping to give up the booze. He has a point.

19. GESTAPO

Back in Belgium, when word came that the Gestapo was going to raid the building where my parents were hiding, my mother left, taking her toothbrush and me. A friend later quipped, "At least she remembered to take you." I laughed, but later thought it a bit unfair to my young mother.

My mother died five years ago, at the age of 97, so I can't ask her where she was going. I will never know. It was one of so many such departures. She probably would not have remembered, even had she been willing to talk about this period in our lives. We probably just moved to whatever room was available and offered at least temporary safety. I have no reason to suppose that it got any easier for them while I was hidden away in the convent, "Au Sacre Coeur." Anyway, I wasn't there very long. The next two years I lived with the De Marneffes, but the occupation wore on, and the deportations continued. My mother never liked to talk about this period in their lives. I did convince her to allow me to interview her on tape once, but she balked, didn't tell me much.

My father, on the other hand, was obsessed with the Holocaust. He routinely reproached me for not knowing and not caring. On one of my visits to their vacation home in Florida, he insisted I read a book about the death camps. We quarreled bitterly. In retrospect, I do realize he wanted me to join him in his pain. My father was an anxious, punctilious man, a stereotypical "yeke," a German Jew, who wouldn't go out to walk the dog without putting on a tie. During the War, he had to hide wherever he could, wear a

Jewish star. He was a physician, and even early on, before *Kristallnacht*, he was not allowed to treat Gentiles. If a non-Jew consulted him, that person could be subject to imprisonment or worse.

But I was talking about my mother and her toothbrush. What would I take out of a burning building? Would I take one of my hundreds of books? What about photographs? Though more portable, digital photographs and books on electronic devices are not that satisfying. Maybe I, too, would take my toothbrush. I would have my memories.

I just heard a talk on the radio about how we all distort our memories, about how our memories are essentially false. Would I want to imagine a new life for myself? I don't think I want to recreate myself, in spite of my constant self-recriminations. In fact, I don't remember much of my childhood. I don't remember my parents during the War, neither the partings nor the reunions. The stories that I heard at home, afterwards, are the sum of my knowledge of that time, that and the photographs I would have had to leave behind.

Does a new language begin a new life? I remember when on the analyst's couch as an adult, I would suddenly speak French or German. No, I don't suffer from Dissociative Identity Disorder with Naomi Black becoming Naomi White. Was I accessing different parts of my life: early childhood, German; middle years, French; adulthood, English with a little Hebrew (from

Ulpan in Israel), a little Spanish (from college)? But nothing stays in its discrete compartment. Our life experiences remain stored in our unconscious, even if the words or conscious memories escape us.

Nowadays, I find myself speaking German out loud to myself, recapitulating my mother's expressions, most of them untranslatable. It feels as though only she could have spoken these phrases with the particular inflections and rhythm. I say to my daughter Genevieve, who speaks German, "Do you remember when she used to say, *Dann haben wir mit Zitronen gehandelt?*" Or, "Whatever did she mean by *ein ekelhaftes Frauenzimmer?*"

In a lot of ways, I am my mother's daughter, but I could never understand her delight in being angry. She would demand that I join her in it, but I couldn't and that made her angrier still. She would berate me, saying, "You never take my side. You don't understand." We would both forget that my expressing anger had been strictly *verboten* while growing up and still as an adult. Neither of my parents could tolerate disagreements or criticisms. My mother reacted with icy anger. My father would tell me that I was 'ridiculous, immature.' Why is it so difficult to talk about the good parts? Maybe because approval and affection were so conditional, so fleeting, not a given. I liked that my mother was smart, funny, tough. She taught me my best curses. She was "people-smart," told stories with the timing of a comedian. I want to inhale those parts of her, but can't get there most of the time, not in any language.

20. NEW YEAR'S EVE

New Year's feels more like an ending than a beginning this year. Maybe it spells the beginning of more loss, of sorrow perhaps. I tend to ignore the dropping of the ball and go to bed before midnight, if possible. I had a patient once, who would curl into bed, early, with a bottle of Scotch, the adult version of mother's milk. I suppose that I am superstitious about looking forward to things in the first place. And well, this year starts badly with a breakup, and promises some difficult times, minor surgery that could go wrong, weeks when I won't be dancing. I do think about making wishes or resolutions. My daughter Genevieve and I performed a ritual one year. You write your wish on a piece of paper, which you then burn. Unfortunately, it didn't occur to me to include the qualifying "fine print" on the piece of paper. Like the character in the story "The Monkey's Paw," I blundered. I wished for a Latin dance partner/lover. He appeared within weeks. He was handsome, charming, a beautiful dancer and a consummate destroyer of my peace of mind. I no longer make wishes.

Should I attempt resolutions? It occurs to me vaguely that I should write more. Maybe meditation should be a path for this year.

"Shoulds" don't really work. I know that. The sentence has to start with "I want." A therapist once suggested writing a list of 100 things I would like to do. The list turned up years later. The first item was "learn to dance Argentine Tango." Voila! This year, on New Year's Day, I drive into Manhattan to dance tango. The drive to TangoMania is easy, except that I keep getting stuck behind drivers even pokier than myself. Maybe they're being cautious after celebrating all night. Somehow, I doubt it. There's parking and I manage to drive into a space, far enough from the bags of garbage on the sidewalk to get out of my car. The mood at the studio is festive. Everyone keeps saying, "Happy New Year." People whom I know only by sight embrace me, as though I were their best friend. Of course, I was trying to ignore the New Year, but New Year's Day is just fine, and I suddenly feel part of the celebration, that we are all friends here at the milonga, at least for the moment. Maybe it's that I am usually alone on the eve of the New Year that makes me want to bury my head under the covers. Tango on January 1st, that's my tradition. Long may it endure!

21. EL DIABLO

Now my adventures! I read someplace that we have parallel existences in which scenarios could play out differently. I like that idea, especially in terms of my Mario tale. I used to think that I was a character in a story he was creating. Sweet revenge! I get to be the author this time.

This all starts with my idea that Barbara should go dancing on her birthday. It is probably the wrong premise to start with. The truth is that I am the one who wants to go dancing. One of my ballroom teachers had given us a list of places to dance. Most of them are too far away, but there is one in Tuckahoe. I make the first fatal error. I call. And a man with a gravelly voice answers. Enter *el Diablo* in sheep's clothing, not quite angel wings. That would be too great a challenge for the costume designer. We get to chatting and I let on that I am looking for a partner for dance practice. Our hero, always quick on the draw, says he knows just the person. He wasn't running any dances, but there was a young man in his 20s, named George, who is always looking for a partner. Now, I am in my late 60s and have confessed this, without giving the exact number, of course. Why would a 20-year-old dance with his grandmother if he had other choices? So, something is amiss. Barbara and I, nevertheless, decide to go, except that Barbara develops back problems… and I'm on my own.

Like all scary and exciting stories, this one begins with it's being dark and rainy. I'm driving up the Hutchinson River Parkway at 40 miles per hour, asking myself, "what on earth am I doing? Shouldn't I have left this man's name and phone number with someone, in case I never return?"

I find the place. It says in large letters, "Mario's Boxing." I don't register that information, as I notice a young man, pacing in front of the place. Head down between stooped muscular shoulders, he looks furtive and nervous. It is obviously the prospective dance partner, George. Immediately, I am challenged by a flight of stairs. I lose my footing at the top and stumble in. I register that Mario, in a muscle shirt, is smiling and has a mustache. Some part of me, no doubt, notices that he is good looking

Half of what looks like a gym is roped off, and muscular young boxers, stripped to the waist, are sparring in the makeshift ring. Later, I learn that with a sink in a corner, the space also serves as a hair salon. There are pin-ups of naked girls in the bathroom. Mario sleeps upstairs in a loft bed that can only be reached by climbing a hanging ladder.

George is a beginner and I relax. Mario starts us off with salsa. Every once in a while, Mario takes over for George. Every once in a while, he disappears into a room adjacent to the gym. I think he's snorting coke. It turns out that he's checking the boxing scores. One of the young guys steps over the rope and wants me to teach him salsa. I am laughing and waiting for Mario to return from shooting up, or whatever else I imagine he's doing, to dance with me again.

George is a good buffer, but it's time for him to go home and he does. The young boxers have drifted out, one of them calling out, "you dance good". Mario takes me through all the dances, wrapping his legs around mine for the tango. I thank him for his generosity, in taking the time to teach me. His talent for nurturance is clear to me when he walks me to my car and asks me to call him when I get home, saying, "I want to make sure you got home safely." I'm so astonished that I return his kiss in the parking lot and that's the beginning of double trouble, but just the beginning.

There is already a message on my tape when I get home. The next day, he says to me, "I was drawn into the vortex of your sensuality. I was smitten." I tell myself that he's eloquent, even if I suspect him of shooting up or other iniquitous acts. Maybe he heard it in a romantic movie. Anyway, you can't look like him and be innocent. By Wednesday, he's calling me three times per day. He's telling me "te quiero." He calls me "mi amor." My college Spanish comes in handy. Is this insane or is it merely "being Spanish"? I'm in a foreign country without a map or passport. I start listening for his voice on my answering machine.

We have a date to go dancing. I ransack my closet for something appropriate to wear. This is at the beginning of my dance craze and I haven't amassed dance clothes yet. So, there I am in an A-line red velvet skirt with gold design bought in a hippie shop in Maine and a black top and flats. I bring my ballroom heeled shoes, but he says that I'm better off in flats. Does it matter what kind of shoes you're wearing when you're moving rhythmically pressed up against somebody's body? Probably not. He turns up nearly on time. The dance studio is downtown, where he's not likely to meet anyone he knows. Besides, there was no one else in the studio, because everyone was off at an Argentine Tango Festival.

He's wearing black jeans, a black button-down shirt and a rakish hat. He's about 5'11, slim-hipped and muscular in arms and shoulders. Don Juan at last! The sexy demon lover: heavy eyebrows, deep-set eyes, quick-witted with a slight derisive smile. He even brings me a single red rose and some fancy chocolates.

22. TO MY FATHER

How sad it is that I was afraid of you. You meant no harm. How could you know what you were doing to me? Your contempt shriveled my heart. I felt brutalized by your insistence that I see the world through your eyes. You wanted to own me. I couldn't breathe. I sidestepped you, as best I could, watching my words, pretending to not go too far from you. I clutched on to my fierce rebellion as to a life raft, whispering: "This is mine, my space! You may not come in. Don't step over that line. Get out! Get Out!"

I moved on. Yet, that leaves me looking for you always, trying to fill an empty space inside me. I am again in love with someone who doesn't truly see me, who wants to toy with me, to declare me his slave.

23. VACATION PLAYGROUND

In the Summer of 1961, I was taking a course at Columbia University, three evenings a week, on the French symbolist Poets. I remember little about it, except that we were to explicate the poems of Mallarmé, Valéry, and Verlaine, under the guidance of Professeur Rifatterre, a dry little man who was missing one ear.

During the day, I worked at a camp called "Vacation Playground," sponsored by the city of New York, overseeing a loosely formed group of teenage girls. With the rock music blaring around me, it didn't take long to realize that speaking to my charges wasn't part of the program. It felt natural to go with the flow and to dance with them.

There was an incident, early on, when two girls went at each other, nails bared. I overheard: "Tu madre es una puta," and found myself jumping into the fray and earning my first scratches in a playground brawl. Mostly, we mindlessly danced with each other. English was a second language with that group. We knew nothing of each other's lives, but the body doesn't lie, and we made friends for the few hours we were together. Dance is simpler and more direct than speech. There are no double messages, no misunderstandings.

At night, with the rock music still pounding in my head, I could make nothing of Mallarmé, of the obfuscations of language, of the arid intellectualism of the course. At another time in my life, I might have appreciated the beauty of the poets' language. That Summer, I was rocking and rolling, living in an alternate universe, while still working towards my degree in Romance Philology and French.

The years when I did free-style dancing at parties or at clubs like Sounds of Brazil, it was exhilarating bonding with others on the dance floor. You might have a partner, but you could mirror and embellish on the moves of other dancers—different from the more formal partner dancing I do now. In Argentine Tango and in Ballroom Dancing, as well, connecting is not optional. Everyone knows, it takes two to tango, but alas, it isn't that easy. Ideally you are totally attuned to your partner and you move as one person, especially when you dance in a close embrace, heart to heart (*corazon a corazon*), as is the common parlance. Of course, there hardly exists a tango song that doesn't have "corazon" and "amor" as part of the lyrics. The man leads, the woman follows. Yes, it sounds sexist, but I have to admit that I am comfortable following and can't imagine leading. As a modern woman, I am often annoyed with myself for following too well, off the dance floor. My friend Samuel teases me that I get things wrong when I don't follow his advice. This is usually in reference to my necessary purchases. He is usually right, but

I feel I follow too slavishly as it is. When it comes to dance, I'm not following anyone's advice really... or is it just that you can't be anyone but yourself when you dance, and that I am, after all, somewhat ambivalent about following? Even in tango, sometimes the woman takes the lead, taking time to do showy steps, communicating her energy and her needs to a receptive partner. I must learn more of these embellishments, these flashy kicks and footwork, called *adornos*, hard to translate into language.

What if you are not in love with your partner? Having a harmonious and passionate connection on the dance floor is a challenge for both partners. Sometimes, you can fake it. When I am lucky, Emil, my tango teacher, asks me to dance, hopefully, for a *tanda*, the typical three dances. If not, someone else might ask me, but decide I am terrible and rudely leave me on the floor after just one dance. With Emil I can stay connected, as he is very strong and skilled in his lead. He doesn't give you much room to go wandering off on your own, away from the moment. And then there is Mario.

24. SAMBA AND SEX

It's all because we are dancing Samba in my living room on a snowy January day that Mario and I have sex for the first time. It's our own version and I could have gone on dancing, instead, for the next hour or so. But he has other ideas, imperatives perhaps, and I have the bad habit of saying "yes," when "no" would have been a better option. So, it happens, "Wham Bam Thank You Ma'am" style with him promising it would get better and wanting to leave right after. He claims he is worried about driving in the snow.

Subsequently, he criticizes *my* performance in bed. What was that about? I have no idea, but he gets a failing grade for finding fault. On the occasion of one of our many breakups, he says: "If it weren't for our phone conversations, I would let it go". On the other hand, it seems to be all about sex for him. He would tell me that since he was Catholic, he felt guilty about sex. My therapist remarked that if it's a sin, it's all the sweeter. Undoubtedly, he felt, at best, ambivalent about his many conquests. "I made them all miserable," he confessed. He should have felt perpetually guilty, but not about the sex, as far as I am concerned.

25. DRIVING DON JUAN

I'm driving Mario and me downtown. He comments with an edge to his voice, "The drivers in back of you are going crazy. You're too slow." I ignore my twinge of discomfort and ask him to drive on the way home. In the process of getting lost on the way to the highway, he asks, "Will you cook for me?" In a moment of lucidity, I say, "Whoa, we just met!" Then I ask the inevitable question, "How old are you?" It turns out he is 50 years old, 18 years younger than I. There and then begins my repeated litany of "this isn't going to work." His usual response is somewhere along the lines of "I'll be over at 7:30 or 8:30 or 10:30" —later and later as the year wears on. Or there are a few days of respite and there we are again. I say to him, "Do you always get what you want?" he responds, "I like to."

Having told him to go away, I sit on my couch leafing through a book, looking at my watch, waiting for him to arrive again. And then he's there. Then he's gone and I wait for the distinctive voice on the phone, a bit hoarse, teasing, seductive. The interval between calls gets longer. I say, "I notice you don't call for a few days after we've had sex." He denies this or asserts, "Oh that's the way I am. It's the way I've always been." Usually after two days or so, I tell myself, "He's not going to call. It's over. That's good." Then he calls.

He takes up where he left off with crude questions such as, "Have you heard of the 82-year-old woman who had sex with a twelve-year-old boy? See! You're never too old!" Then it's, "Come to my place tonight. I'll give you a lesson in quickstep". It's Thursday and he wants to have sex, sometime after ten p.m. I tell him I'm tired and he says, "Ah, come on" or, "Don't be such a baby. I got up to work at five a.m." He is of course always "working" on the weekends or "with his children." He leaves me messages telling me that he's "hot." He tells me that he has a fantasy about going among throngs of people and of blessing everyone. I can't help thinking that it would be a mistake to cast him as Jesus in one of those casts of thousands Hollywood productions. He also tells me that he is superior to other people: "They are all ants," he declares. Sometimes he recites Romeo's soliloquy to Juliet on the phone message. Mostly he talks about sex, anyway he can, through jokes, anecdotes, innuendo and open invitation. I save his messages on my tape machine and listen to them over and over.

When I confront him about his behavior, he listens, but tells me I am wrong, totally wrong, and that I distort what he says and does. He says, "Look at the retarded couples. They hold hands. They love each other. They don't play games." He tells me, "I love you and I hate you." He wants to know if I love him more than any man in the world.

All this goes on from January to January, one year, more or less. December 20th is the day when I'm able to say with absolute conviction, "this is over." A few weeks before I said goodbye forever, he had sold his car and it was up to me to do all the driving to see him.

I would find myself wondering what I was doing there. Often, I would retreat to my car to listen to music and to consider driving away.... but in the end, I would stay while he finished up with his students or boxers. The dance lesson is usually mercifully short. I climb up the swinging ladder to his loft bed, not an inconsiderable challenge for arthritic knees, and we make love in total darkness. At night all cats are gray, I imagine he is thinking. But, "Ah, bliss!"

The evening of my final epiphany, I prepare to go to a dance in Connecticut at a place called "Let's Dance" as I am absolutely certain Mario does not want to see me. It is, after all, Saturday night and he's more a Thursday night late-night-tryst kind of guy. Ours is what he calls "an unconventional kind of relationship."

I am to meet my friend Amanda this night at the dance, as she is having her own romantic crisis. "Let's Dance" is well-known among ballroom dancers. It is a large, somewhat bleak gym, lined with benches for the many single women and a few slouching, uncommunicative men. The more attractive men are up and dancing, taking their pick of the younger, better dancers. Amanda is due to arrive late. I sit down to put on my ballroom shoes, look up and see... "el Diablo," as large as life, sitting right next to me.

At first, I don't even register that it's him. I'm in shock and say, "Should one of us go home?" He responds blithely, not looking at me, "Oh no, there are plenty of seats and plenty of people to dance with. I didn't come to dance with you, and you didn't come to dance with me". With that, he's off searching for other partners. He puts his arms around a voluptuous redhead for a fox trot. I have to leave.

I go to the vestibule to change from ballroom shoes into flats and to put on my coat.

I'm putting on my coat, when I remember Amanda. Amanda is counting on me to be there. I try to call her on my cell phone. She's unreachable. I put the heels back on and go back into the ballroom. I see him dancing with a tall blonde. Run back out to change into my flats. Try to call Amanda again. No luck. Okay. I'm back in the ballroom with my heels on. He's giving the blonde a hug and walking her back to her seat. So, it's back out to the vestibule, shivering a bit, as it's cold. Still no Amanda. I give up and decide to tough it out. About that time, Amanda finally arrives, full of her own bad news.

She exclaims, "Naomi, you look like a little wild animal. I thought someone attacked you. I thought you were going to jump out of the window." Luckily there are no windows and I'm laughing and crying at her rant. She keeps saying, "Listen to me. You're supposed to listen to me tonight." I point Mario out to her. She says, "Well, he sure can dance." Then she catches herself and says, "He's a goon. He's a lounge lizard. He doesn't care about you. This is good. Now you know what he's like!"

This of course is all news to me! A lounge lizard? What a come down! No, of course he's not! But still, I want to leave. She says to me, "You are staying right here". I remind myself that I look good tonight. I look around me for partners, smiling at each with whatever élan I can muster. Maybe I can make him sweat a little too. Our lounge lizard dances with me just once. He throws me around and has a conversation with someone over my shoulder, never making eye contact with me.

But by 8:15 Monday morning, he has called three times. I screen the first two. The first one is something like, "Hey, party girl, did you have a good time?" The second one is some kind of silly joke. I pick up the third call and tell him, "I don't like you anymore. We are through". He calls three more times that day. This goes on for the next three months with some interruptions. I screen all my calls. This is before caller i.d., and I listen to every message. There are several claiming to be from the "Indian Guru, Chupak," urging peace. Then on another call the Guru counsels, "You should go to an Ashram for two months and chant Om." What I don't hear is an apology, not that it would affect my resolution to never speak to him again.

I wait for the withdrawal symptoms to go away. I can't help smiling at some of the goofy messages. I save some of them and guiltily replay them. After a while he sounds a bit worried, "I haven't talked to you in three weeks. Have you skipped town?" Did he completely disbelieve me when I said that we were through? He keeps behaving as though nothing has happened, assuming that I will join him in his delusion. More than anything, I fear weakening.

During this time, I still have fantasies about him, although I know that the Mario I imagine does not exist. I congratulate myself on my clear headedness, but my favorite fantasy is where he says he can't live without me and begs for forgiveness, all in the context of doing the tango with me. I know, I know, his "love" lasts about 3 minutes when it surfaces. Ah, love, I was never so miserable in my whole life. I am not going to pick up that phone. He skips a few days and then a week or two. I miss the calls.

My mother, who enjoys this adventure more than I, at this point says, "I bet you $500 that he's going to call again." I suggest, "How about $5? I don't want to be poor, as well as miserable." He does call, but at less frequent intervals, with less colorful messages. Three months into this, I impulsively pick up the phone and it's him. He says, "You knew it was me." "I counter, "No, I didn't." Alas, phone conversations are a slippery slope. I want a truce, but I don't want to fall back into his clutches. Through these months, I make up speeches in my head, explaining it all to him. Now I write him a letter that should clarify why I can't be with him.

In my letter, I tell him that he is toying with me, that he doesn't see me as a real person, that he doesn't even like me. I don't remember the rest of it. I just remember his telling me, "It was a good letter, but none of it is true!"

26. FATHER

I remember being in my parents' cream-colored Cadillac on the way to South Hampton Hospital, where my father lay dying. My mother was driving. She told me that the day before my father kept collapsing to the floor. His legs couldn't seem to hold him up-right, as though the connection between the brain and his limbs had been severed. She had called an ambulance. We are both calm on this trip to the hospital, where my father used to be an attending physician and where now he was most likely going to die. There are still nurses at the hospital who remember him, although he is nearly 95 years old and had stopped practicing many years ago. My mother says, "I just want him to be comfortable." She tells me how his lips turned blue twice before the ambulance came and how he fought being put on the stretcher. I feel nothing. I imagine him erect, in a dark suit, the eyes sharp behind round wire-rimmed glasses, but giving some hints of vulnerability or diffidence if you looked closely. It's a photograph of him I remember. He is dancing with me at my wedding. He's wearing a yarmulke; he looks stern. We dance the waltz together, he, tall and proud; I, smiling in my white lace, princess-for-a-day wedding gown, with my hair swept up and the long train to my dress pinned up.

For the past year my father has been increasingly demented. He doesn't recognize my mother, refuses to get into their bed at night, insisting, "I don't sleep with strange women." One day he calls me and says cheerfully, "We have a visitor," meaning my mother. Another time he calls and says sadly, "Please send your mother home. Tell her that we have cake." This breaks my heart. Other times he demands that he be allowed to go home, finding nothing familiar in his surroundings. When I visit, he stares through me, as though I were invisible. Sometimes he looks at me, puzzled. When I hold his hand, it is ice cold. On my last visit, he paces wildly, moving from chair to chair with manic energy. Who is this skinny personage who barely resembles my father? He eats avidly, whatever happens to be on the table. This is after a lifetime of exercising iron control over his diet. Sometimes he chews on the napkins. He hallucinates cars on the opposite wall.

My mother and I arrive at the hospital on this cold, brisk March morning. It is sunny and silent. We get lost in the maze of hospital corridors. It is very clean. There are no smudges on the freshly painted white and green walls. It smells of disinfectant. We find my father writhing on his hospital bed. His eyes are closed. He doesn't see anything or anyone. He has unlearned speech. We don't know if he hears anything. My mother goes up to him and strokes his arm. He flinches away from her touch. I, too, should go up to him, say something, just not touch him. I don't want to go near him, but I do. He rears away as though in pain. It is a stranger on that bed. I wonder if he's afraid. I wonder if he's wrestling with death, whether he fights going under. I hope that the thrashing around is just reflexive. We don't stay very long, not even a half hour. I follow my mother's lead. She hires a nurse to sit with him all day and all night. I feel that we are wrong to leave so promptly, but I am relieved. We're hungry. He is dying and we're hungry. We go to the Hospital coffee shop. My mother orders a turkey sandwich. I have tuna fish. With lettuce on rye. It's good to be sitting with my mother, the two of us out to lunch, something we never do.

That night my mother invites me to ransack her shoe collection with her. I remember from my teen years that she often bought shoes that were too small for her and then gave them to me. I especially remember a pair of red spiked high heels. There is nothing like that in her current collection, as she is now 87 years old. She is irritated with Virginia, my father's aide, but decides to invite her to join us anyway to pick out any shoes she likes from my mother's discards. Virginia, Eastern European immigrant, tall, blond, and patient, lives in a small simple room in the house. It has some bookshelves with books in German and in English, a Degas reproduction of a dancer leaning over to adjust the lace of her toe shoe, and a photograph of my paternal grandparents, austere and European in black and white. The three of us women have a shoe fest. There is almost a holiday atmosphere tonight.

Later that night, I am half asleep and I hear my mother moving around. I see her coming out of the bedroom she has shared with my father for 65 years. Her large body is naked, and she is unsteady on her feet. She's very old without her dentures and without her wig. It gives me a shock to see her like that. She leans on me, making her slow way to the bathroom. She sits on the toilet, looks sadly into my eyes, and says: "Why do you always tell me I am ugly? Why do you never tell me, I am pretty?" I feel terror in the pit of my stomach. I think to myself, "Now my mother is demented too!" But I am struck by the sadness of the question, which is no doubt addressed to my absent father. Being "beautiful" has always been of primary importance to my mother, and she was beautiful and, in a way, still is, with her large hazel eyes and regular features. "Yes, you are pretty," I say to her as I lead her to the empty bed. I fall back asleep and I wake up from a nightmare about a dog. My parents had a German shepherd, which my mother adored. She prefers animals to people, she often says. All her charities, especially when my father is gone and can no longer ridicule her, are to animal shelters and rescue operations. Through the years, both my father and I somewhat resent the dog and I have never worked up much enthusiasm for animals. In the nightmare, an ugly, grey haired, foul smelling German Shepherd is about to jump on my face.

At 7 a.m., the phone rings. Virginia picks it up and gets the news that my father died at five a.m. that morning. Both my mother and Virginia cry briefly. At the memorial, the living room overflows with friends and neighbors of my parents'. My mother doesn't care about this, but I insist someone say Kaddish. We survived the holocaust in occupied Belgium. Though none of us is an observant Jew, it seems appropriate and I crave some ritual, to mark his death. An elderly friend obliges in an uncertain quavering voice. He, later that afternoon, asks my mother out to dinner. She is indignant about this and refuses. My mother has turned to ice. She barely looks at me, doesn't touch me, doesn't allude to the words I have spoken for my father. There is an abyss between us. Her words to me are bitter and dismissive. I, too, freeze in response and keep my distance. In what I always call her "dead fish voice," she says repeatedly, "You don't understand." She tells people, in my presence, "Now I am alone. I have no one."

27. THE BLACK HOLE OF TANGO

One of my ballroom partners was fond of saying that people disappear into the black hole of tango. I still keep one foot in the ballroom world, but, yes, there is a "black hole" that pulls you in. And I love tango. But, getting partners at a milonga is a problem, especially as I long to dance every dance. My tango teacher's point of view is that you are not going to be asked unless you are really hot or an excellent dancer. So, for me, obviously, the only option is to become an excellent dance, for how hot can you be at the age of 75? That means more private lessons with Emil. We get into the groove of weekly lessons. Of course, there is no tango teacher in all of New York City who knows how to teach tango, except for him. He teaches close embrace and I learn *volcadas, colgadas, giros, ganchos,* etc. Sometimes he tells me I am fabulous, and he loves my energy. Sometimes it's, "What's that? That's not tango. You are doing samba." I am not quite fabulous enough to get asked to dance a lot. Nevertheless, Emil insists I come to more milongas. For me that means driving one hour in traffic to watch other people dance while mulling over the fact that I am neither hot, nor an excellent dancer. One week, as an incentive, Emil decides that we are going to celebrate "Ms. Silver's" birthday at the *Silver* Ballroom. He says, "Everyone will dance with you. I'll bring cake. I am going to perform too, so you have to come." So, of course I go. I am the first one there and I feel self-conscious, wandering around the empty room. All these things start at least an hour later than announced and it is gauche to come so early. The milonga doesn't start till ten p.m., which to me is a realistic time to start the long trek home. This time I stay. I don't know a soul, but I have to at least watch Emil's performance. At 11:30, everyone is told to sing "happy birthday." Then the men are told to dance with me, one after another. Some comply. Others forgo the pleasure. I know that I am dancing badly, as a few seconds with a series of strangers isn't enough to catch on to anyone's style. Before I leave at 1 a.m., I congratulate Emil on his performance. At the next lesson, he asks me whether I was there for the show. He accuses me of lying when I tell him that I most definitely was there. Then he tells me, "You danced horrible. I saw you. You danced tango to vals music." I am abashed and think that I can never return to that particular milonga. But I do think that Emil needs some assistance with pedagogical techniques. I suggest that instead of telling me that I was horrible, he could say, "Your vals needs work." He smiles at me impishly and says, "Come on, I didn't mean no harm."

28. IT TAKES TWO

Emil now has added a Stage Tango Group to his offerings. It runs for six weeks and then you perform. I did perform with him once, in Westchester, where he was teaching at that time. I had been taking lessons with him for about four months. As we prepared for my first tango performance ever, he moaned, "If only you knew even ten percent of the technique." I offered to cancel my first appearance as a tango dancer, but he decided to go through with it. At the dress rehearsal, one hour before the performance, he told me I was wearing the wrong dress. "This is a flamenco dress," he said. I offered to take off the red flowers, but he reassured himself, "Never mind, no one knows anything about tango here anyway." In the event, I was "fabulous" and everyone loved my "flamenco dress."

But this time it's different. I have to find a partner to be in the show. This turns out to be daunting. Getting a man to ask me for a dance and to stay for the whole *tanda* (3 dances usually) is hard enough. It's all because I am old. Emil makes no secret of this. He tells me that he has asked three separate men and that they all have declined to dance with me. When I suggest that he might have spared me that information, he says, "One is too old, one is too young, and one is a jerk." I am left to figure out which of the men at the studio rejected me. I have a pretty good idea, which doesn't dispose me favorably towards these particular men. Too bad for them, when I get to be an "excellent dancer." Miracle of miracles, he does find me a partner. I expect someone fat, ugly, clumsy, disagreeable. Miguel turns out to be handsome, very polite and a professional dancer. He and Emil have known each other for ten years and he often comes to the milongas to help with the gender gap. I give him credit for his courtliness. He makes sure to dance at least once with women who are neither "hot" nor "excellent dancers." We do two shows together. The other women look at me enviously and I say silently, to myself, "Stay away from him, please." We like each other and dance together whenever we end up at the same milonga. Still, keeping my jealousy in check when he so much as talks to another woman seems to be challenging. My curfew gets later, but I do have to make the midnight shuttle to my train home. Thank you, Emil!!

29. TROUBLE IN TANGO PARADISE

Just when everything was going so well with my new tango partner, Emil messes with the works. Miguel tells me, "Emil has banned me from all his workshops and milongas. He thinks I am stealing students from him." He will simply dance at other milongas. That's all very sensible, but what am I going to do? When I confront Emil about this, he goes into a rant, "What's the matter with you? You're sick in the head. Why do you take his part, not mine? Are you in love with him? He has been handing out cards and he promised to stop. If I didn't have respect, I would have kicked his ass, in front of everyone." Kick his ass? Miguel is slender and fine-boned, and Emil is tall and stocky, more like a prize fighter than a dancer. But fortunately, Emil is all talk, and plenty of it. I've had ample opportunity to test out the veracity of his stories, so I go with Miguel's version. Nothing much changes for Emil, except that the gender gap has, of course, increased. Two or three women for every man is routine. Emil can't dance fast enough to make all of the women, or even most of the women, including myself, happy at any given milonga.

Still, he continues to periodically ask me to fund a studio for him. He says, "You could have your name up in lights and you could go to all the milongas for free." His timing couldn't be worse. I miss Miguel and I complain to Emil that there is no one for me to dance with. He still insists I come and wait to, at best, be asked to dance by someone with two left feet, or to sit and watch others dance. Sometimes, I leave early and, often, in tears. Perhaps Emil feels somewhat responsible for the situation, perhaps not. In any case, he suggests that I hire someone: "Hire a taxi dancer," he says. I take him at his word and meet with Miguel, to suggest an arrangement. I tell Emil, who says: "Good for you, have a good time, but don't bring him to my milongas." A day later, the day of his Friday milonga, he has thought better of it. Now he insists I call Miguel and ask him to come that very night. Since I am not about to do this, he has no choice but to make the call himself. Miguel who prefers peace, comes, just to say hello. Emil embraces the prodigal son and we toast the occasion with Emil's wine. In private, Emil insists: "I don't care about Miguel. I did it for you, because you are fabulous."

The jubilation is short lived as Emil gets reports that Miguel and I have been seen dancing at other milongas, "all night." Sometimes Miguel isn't free on the night of Emil's milonga and I prefer to go with him. This is intolerable. Why don't I come to his milongas by myself and wait to get asked, like the other girls? He continually comments that now that I'm paying him, Miguel has to dance all the time, that I am squeezing him dry. He makes sure I understand that I wouldn't get to dance much, if I weren't paying someone. I confide in Miguel, leaving out the part about Emil's" kicking his ass" and my being in love with him. He calmly suggests that I should get whatever I can from the lessons and ignore the rest. Very sensible advice, I am sure. We will dance on the weekend, regardless of Emil's spies.

Miguel has many female admirers. When he introduces me to a young Asian woman, she breaks out in a wide smile, her voice goes up an octave and she says, "He is the sweetest man and the best dancer." Some version of this I hear repeated any number of times. I have to agree. But I am supposed to give up dancing with him, to please my teacher, talented though he may be. Emil again says the following week, "Why do you always come with your boyfriend? Are you in love with him?" He refers to Miguel as my "boyfriend" in ever more contemptuous tones. He suggests I hire the "Chinese guy." Then I could have two boyfriends. Clearly something is amiss!! We have a strange kind of triangle and I search my mind for indications of Emil's possible sexual interest in me. He is given to extravagant gestures, but always when Miguel is present. He will clasp me in his arms and say fervently, "You know I adore you from my heart." To my great amusement, when the mood takes him, he looks intensely into my eyes. "Here is the drama and passion of tango," he seems to be telegraphing before holding me in the typical close embrace, maybe a bit more tightly than necessary. Sometimes I play along and give him a passionate look. Or else, while showing me a step, he will murmur seductively, "What's your name. I want to take you out to dinner." I will respond, Lola or Anastasia, whatever comes into my head. He often expresses his approval of what I'm wearing by saying suggestively, "Excuse *me*...!" It's all meant in good fun, I guess, even when he pinches me when I am dancing with Miguel. I have no doubt that Emil has no interest in older women like me. He likes to play. Maybe he enjoys the scenario of winning over a rival. After all, there has to be blood on the floor for tango. Miguel, for his part is a perfect gentleman and focuses entirely on the dance. When I ask if Miguel can join me for my lessons, he agrees with alacrity, but in classic Emil style, he informs me that he charges more for couples.

When Miguel and I take lessons with Emil, the men are polite with each other. Sometimes they call each other "maestro." There has to be drama though! This is a golden opportunity for Emil, to make sure we understand how tango is a dangerous dance. He warns Miguel, if you lean that way, she's going to lose balance, she's going to fall. He says to me, "You do that, he's going to kick you." Turning to Miguel, he says, "She wants you to kick her. She wants you to hurt her." Brandishing an imaginary whip, he goes on, "You know that some women, they like to be hurt. They're, what do you call it? Masochists." Oy, what a vivid imagination! Miguel, laughing a little, protests "I am not a violent man."

So, this goes on in a similar vein, except that Emil ups the ante. He keeps asking me to put him in my will. Is he going to put a hit on me, if I do? One day, he asks a leading question, "Is Miguel in your will?" I wish I had said: "Now, that's an interesting idea! Let me think about that." I don't know how all this is going to end. Will I at least get to be an excellent tango dancer? Maybe we're going to have to have a threesome, Emil, Miguel and me. Really, Emil just likes to play. And it is all a part of the drama of tango. There's bound to be a sequel, unless I stop dancing or go to learn from one of the many teachers who have no idea how to teach tango.

30. DANCE HOSTS

It is customary to reserve a table for the social at the Starlight Ballroom. Usually, Miguel calls and our little table has a paper sign saying, "Miguel G.- 2." We're usually in the same place, one row away from the dance floor. Single women are placed in front, where they can be seen and so be more likely to be asked to dance. When I used to go dancing by myself, I tended to stand, in some conspicuous place, to be super ready. Ideally, I want to dance every dance. It isn't all that helpful to be sitting with a whole clutch of women, sort of hidden.

The table next to ours has four people. As the evening wears on, I see that one older woman, wearing a tailored white dress, sits at the table by herself most of the time. It's a terrible feeling when no one asks you to dance, I tell Miguel. He says, "Do you want me to dance with her?" He doesn't look enthused at the prospect and we rationalize that she will know we felt sorry for her and that would be humiliating. Also, we want to do this last foxtrot together.

He says that if he were in that situation, he would hire someone, even if it was just for once a month. Of course, Miguel would never face that problem. He is handsome and a lovely dancer. As a man, it's his role to ask and any woman would be eager to dance with him. A woman needs a certain amount of moxie to ask. Tonight, it seems to me as though everyone is there with a paid host. There's Miriam with her new young, slim partner. He's affectionate with her, leans into her, strokes her hair. She seems happy, even smiles at me, though she seems mostly to ignore women. Tony, who used to dance with her, is there with Sara. Miguel thinks that both men might be gigolos, not necessarily with their current partners. I say, "But Tony is gay." He says, "All the better. You don't have to compete with other women." I think, "But of course, there are other men."

Suddenly. I remember my mother's friend, Stephie, in her eighties when I knew her. She had befriended two young gay men, who lived in her building in Inwood. The three of them would go out to dinner, to shows, hang out together, talk. She was obsessed with them, was desolate when they broke up, but made friends with the new boyfriend. They formed the center of her life and my mother's eyes would glaze over with boredom, as she endlessly extolled their virtues and accomplishments and shared the latest news about their lives. Undoubtedly, they were the children she never had and the imaginary lovers, whom we desire at any age. Sometimes we settle for fantasy. If we are lucky, we get to do a sexy rumba with an attractive man, a mini-love affair on the dance floor.

31. RAIN

I rarely listen to the weather, so I am alarmed when I find the West Side Highway flooded on my way downtown one evening. I take deep breaths to calm myself, as I edge my car carefully along the road. I shouldn't have gone, even if I did allow an extra 45 minutes to find parking. It is Saturday night and I am heading for midtown. I am prepared to turn my car around and go home if nothing materializes in that time. Now, to make things worse, it is raining buckets. My cell phone is plugged in so that I can reach it easily to speed-dial Miguel to tell him I am not going to make it. I am rehearsing in my mind the words, "Forget Emil's Saturday milonga for the foreseeable future. Even once per month is too often."

But I make steady progress, make a wrong turn, and find a parking space one block from the diner at which I am to meet Miguel—and I am early. Whoever said that anticipatory anxiety does no good at all? I didn't get into an accident *and* I found parking! I do have to check that the space is actually legal. That means getting out of the car and reading the signs. I reach into the back seat to find the umbrella. There is no umbrella and no, there isn't a small one in the glove compartment. I rush out of the car, open the trunk and grab a DiCicco's shopping bag to hold over my head and read the sign that will tell me whether I need to anticipate a $100 parking fee or even worse, having my car towed. The sign says—and I read it twice, in spite of the pelting rain—"Commercial Vehicles Only: Three-hour Parking Monday-Friday." It's Saturday, so it's o.k. I start speed walking under my grocery bag. Now it's coming down in torrents. I hug the walls, hoping for an awning of some sort. There are, after all, hotels around here. When I get to the Avenue, I see a souvenir shop and rush in. Yes, they do have umbrellas for $8. The sign says, "Returns only within seven days". I am shivering a bit, very wet and frozen. I open my new purchase and walk half a block to the diner, where, of course, it is air conditioned. Whoever heard of being cold in the Summer? I order hot decaffeinated tea and hold my hands around the cup. Miguel is late. He was smart and waited out the worst of the storm under a doorway. So why couldn't I have stayed in my car for an extra ten minutes? It's no longer raining but, in spite of the sign in the window, I am pretty sure the store will not give me a refund on my lightly used umbrella. I am wearing the two-piece purple dress that Natalya made for me and I know it will dry quickly, not so my velvet jacket or my sandals. I have forgotten my book and I try to interest myself in the ball game broadcast on the TV screens placed strategically so that customers can watch while eating their dinners, or in my case, drinking their tea. I manage to figure out that the Chicago Orioles are playing the New York Yankees and that the Orioles are the ones in the orange uniforms. Finally, Miguel arrives and orders a Stella Light. He's more talkative than usual tonight. I like that. He even laughs a bit. When we get to the milonga, I am still chilled, and I discover that the pain pads on my feet are floating free in my sodden nylons. They are useless and I remove them. I haven't left the house with "unpadded" feet in months. How am I going to dance? Also, I wish I had another pair of hose or even peds. No, peds wouldn't do anyway. The skirt has high slits and you don't display naked thighs at my age, unless you're at the beach and have no choice. My feet hurt immediately in my thin-soled dance shoes. I tell Miguel that I might not be able to dance for very long. "Not even an hour?" he asks. I am thinking, probably not. It hurts getting through the first two dances, so he suggests drinking a little wine. Another dancer pours me a third of a small paper cup of white wine, warning me that it tastes metallic, but I like it fine. Before I know it, I feel no pain at all. I feel really happy, entranced by the music and the other dancers; the women in their various fetching outfits, the sexy glide of the tango. I am in love with everyone and everything in my fuzzy altered state. It gets to be 11:30 p.m. and Miguel is ready to leave. I could have danced another hour, even more. But somewhere in the recesses of my mind a small voice whispers that it is time to go home. So, I walk out with him, wanting more, not wanting the night to end, always wanting more.

32. BAD DREAMS

My alarm clock is aging out. It no longer has the rambunctious timbre of earlier years. I hear it only when I am awake. It should be discarded. But really, should you discard an old friend, or is it an enemy? Besides I can't figure out a newer model, because I, too, am old. Yes, though it is true, it is a lame excuse. How about taking the time to read the directions with any kind of thoroughness? It isn't happening.

This morning I wake up at nine a.m. with the clock whining in the background, barely audible. It was set to wring me out of sleep at eight, so this means a hectic start to the day. My nights have been restless this week, filled with bad dreams. At 3:30 this morning, after tossing in my bed in pain, I take a Tylenol and half of my muscle relaxant. Earlier in the week, it's a question of avoiding reliving a repetitive dream that propels me out of bed before dawn. In the dream, I am desperately trying to get in touch with my daughter Julie. No one will give me her phone number. She is out of reach, though we are presumably in the same hotel and, in dream logic, she may or may not have reached Broadway safely and I am somewhere on the East side. This scenario seems out of all proportion disturbing to me. This so much so, that I remain wrapped in fog through the first part of my dance lesson that day. Alexey says, "Naomi, where are you? You're wandering around like an abandoned child." It occurs to me that being lost can be much like being left behind. My eyes fill with tears.

Probably the intensity of my terror indicates that this is a reliving of my early separation from my parents. Being surrounded by fog or snow (and it was snowing) has evolved for me into a metaphor for being isolated and not being able to reach anyone, nor give voice to my fear and loneliness. There have been so many dreams about cut phone lines, about being incommunicado, not being able to find my way home.

Lately most of those dreams have been directly about my parents. Besides the early separations, there were so many failures to connect emotionally in real life. I remember standing huddled in the rain at the small cemetery where my mother was buried. She was 97 years old. When she was dying, she could no longer speak, expressed herself only in moans. At the burial, I found myself speaking to her half in English half in German. I don't know to what end, but I tell her we should have had more conversations. The last thing she said to me in a moment of lucidity, was, "I am sorry. I couldn't do any better." I wonder now whether I failed her too. Her last few months, she had shrunk to a tiny body, making sounds that terrified me. She no longer resembled my mother. When I took her hand on one of my visits, and tried to lie down with her, she dug her nails into my hand and shouted out loud in German, "Go." There was a movie I saw called *Amour*, where the dying woman also moaned continuously as she lay dying. I could hardly bear to watch it. I was spared much of this horror, as I lived relatively far away and my mother's patient and kind aide, Geraldine, and her long-term employee, but really adopted family, Laura of the generous heart and immense common sense, bore the brunt. There were few of us at the Memorial after the dispiriting rain-drenched event at the Cemetery. Geraldine and Laura, both with tears in their eyes, were most lavish in their praise, talking of her generosity, wisdom, kindness. I don't remember much else of what was said except for my ex-husband's saying, "and she was so beautiful." When I was a toddler, I thought her the most beautiful woman in the world, but she was so much more.

How do you sort out what you want to internalize about a complicated and in many ways unfulfilled woman? My mother, who, brought up in wealth and luxury, just escaped being deported by the Nazis, who experienced hunger and fear and gratefully washed other people's dishes in the safe kitchen of rich employers in the U.S. after the war? Yes, of course, that inheritance is mine, but it is vastly complicated.

Lately, I have been trying to own my connection with my now deceased parents, conjuring up their endearing qualities and the sense of familiarity that doesn't exist with anyone else. Like it or not, you know them in a special way, you belong to them, to the family myths, to the family routines, to their vulnerabilities, to the jokes, to the brooding angers, to the memories, to the losses. The languages, the 'familiar' almost-forgotten treats bring up memories, if only gustatory. I see *stollen* in the supermarket and think about buying a loaf, though nobody likes it. A catalogue of holiday goodies is dropped into my mailbox. They are still offering the seven-layer chocolate cake, which was a favorite, though the petits fours were always disappointing. I think about my father and his sense of mischief, how he loved chocolate, just as I do, of course. I used to like to hear the old stories again and again. I don't know why. Perhaps because reminiscence meant a thaw in the on and off family cold war.

My father liked to tell how he and his sister were sometimes given a chocolate bar as children. He would eat his right away and then make short work of his sister's, who had carefully wanted to save hers. I remember after dementia had engulfed him, his sitting at the dining room table eating all the chocolate that had been set out for guests and my mother's rushing to salvage some of it and save him from indigestion.

But back to my dreams: they are predictably bad. I have a friend with a history similar to mine, who always dreams of beautiful landscapes. Maybe he's not telling about the bad ones. Maybe the trees and flowers have hidden menace. He was hidden on a farm when he was three and four, surrounded by the Nazi peril. It does seem to me that his relationships with people are off kilter. Then again, he hasn't struggled through years of therapy. His solution perhaps is to be oblivious to his inner life. Are my tortured night-longings preferable? In French and in Spanish they call a sleepless night a "white night." Yes, I end up in a white cocoon when awakened from my nightmares. Still, I imagine forgiving my parents their absence.

33. SHOAH

Yesterday I started to watch a video of my father's interview with Shoah in 1997. He is 90 years old and keeps apologizing for his poor memory. His English is halting in a way I don't associate with him. Both my parents spoke English well, but of course with a German accent. I remember a lot of the stories of near miraculous escapes from the Gestapo. The Belgians called them "les sales Boches," which can loosely be translated as "the dirty Krauts." What was missing then and now in the interview is a sense of the terror that pervaded our lives. My father smiles and laughs a little when sharing some horrific story. He seems more subdued when he talks of my hiding experience in the convent. He says, of seeing me when they came to visit and ultimately took me out, "She was completely changed. She was very disturbed." In general, though, it is all seen from a great distance. I think that I too experienced it, at least consciously, from the same remove.

When I went to see the film *Woman in Gold*, I didn't expect much footage of the S.S., though the film revolved around the restitution to its owner of a painting by Klimt, stolen by the Nazis. I found myself crying from the beginning to the end of the movie, starting when I heard the protagonist speaking German at her sister's grave. She said simply, "Goodbye, my dear sister." It's about a cultivated family in Vienna. The sound of pounding of the Gestapo's boots on their doorstep makes me imagine the terror of the occupation for my young parents in a visceral way.

34. DON JUAN REDUX

I discover a local dance which I like. One night I walk in and I see George. My heart sinks. That means that Don Juan is here. George is of course the driver, now that Mario doesn't have a car. I see him. It seems to me he looks a bit seedy tonight. He hasn't shaved and he may have put on a few pounds. He's wearing some kind of dorky, print polyester shirt. Maybe he's not even up to being a credible lounge lizard. If he cleaned up, he would make a good gigolo, except that he couldn't be compliant enough, even for money. Hurrah, I'm over him. In a maneuver that becomes typical for the next several months, he walks towards me, as though I were invisible, and asks the woman standing in back of me or next to me to dance. I work at not seeing him and looking as though I were having a great time, dancing with often fat, balding, clumsy men. Sometimes I catch him watching me.

Sometimes he doesn't come and I'm relieved, but a bit disappointed. There are times that I take the long drive into the city and go to another dance venue to avoid this situation.

One night, in the middle of the year, he follows me out of the dance, dismissing George. He says, "I'm walking you to your car. It's dangerous around here." Of course, he's the only dangerous thing in sight. He grabs me to kiss me. I fight him off …unsuccessfully. He says, "The magic is still here." I tell myself that I'm really angry.

He calls the next morning, saying, "Thank you for last night." Other nights, I give in and ask myself, what I am doing. To my rhetorical question, "Why am I doing this?" he says, "Because it feels good." I can't argue with that.

I am dazzled by the magic of his returning. I asked him once if he could ever stand still long enough to allow anyone to love him. He says "No, it is too late." He complains that I am never the first to say, "I love you." I remind him that if I did so, he would run away as fast as he could. He doesn't argue. He knows it is true. He plays at love, like a child with a favorite toy, teasing, caressing, making me laugh, cajoling, sticking a knife between my ribs. I can't resist him. My efforts to send him away are half-hearted. I feel torn apart whenever I leave him.

My therapist says, "Why do you tell him anything? He doesn't listen anyway." She says that I should think about my father, that this non-relationship replicates the earlier father-daughter dynamics. What?? My father would have hated this lout! He is a Latino dancer/boxer/hairdresser and he is 18 years younger than I. Oh yes, he also was an actor. He doesn't read much, but his sharp intelligence and his wicked sense of humor keep me engaged. Yes, okay, he is sexy too and super seductive.

I learn to look for his shadow when I leave the dance, hoping and fearing that he is following me. One night he taps on the window of my car as I am innocently eating a protein bar for the trip home. I open the door to the passenger seat. He tells me that he has changed; I know he hasn't changed, but I kiss him anyhow.

"I want to resume our relationship," he says. I ask myself, "What relationship? We talked on the phone. We had sex. Sometimes we watched a movie on my bed, well one half or maybe a third of a movie." In disbelief, I hear him saying, "I lost the best relationship I ever had, and I've learned." My mind is saying, "No way!!" The rest of me is saying, "Bring it on." Anyway, I do say "no" to this scheme. I tell him in the fullness of my wisdom, "You know it's just going to end up the same way." Later he will say, "You haven't changed. I've changed; you haven't. I don't want to be tortured anymore." This I do understand!

The next morning, there's a message: "Thank you for last night. It was like old times. You should come down here so we can discuss our relationship. You're resisting. It's not healthy."

When we next talk on the phone, I ask, "Why should I come to see you, when you won't talk to me in public?" He says, "I see I'm going to have to dance with you. I will forge a relationship with you at the dance." Sure enough, as soon as I arrive, he invites me to dance. We dance tango, smooth and sexy. He stops towards the end and asks, "Are you coming to my place tonight?" I say, "I don't think so." He drops my hand and says, "In that case, I don't have to dance with you." With that he glides away to a better prospect. When I talk to him in a few weeks (Oh, why would I?), I say, "So, you won't talk to me unless I have sex with you?" He says, "Well everything is quid pro quo in life." He is right, of course, but why does he have to be so crass?!

So, when he repeatedly asks me to not only be his sex partner, but his exclusive sex partner, I say "no." "Exclusive" is a big concession for Don Juan. Nevertheless, I say, "No, I can't do that." Finally, I have wised up.

There is no news for months. Then one day, there is a message in that gravelly voice: "I can't imagine why I'm calling this den of iniquity!" But I don't pick up or even want to. I know now that it's over. He told me that I would never get over him. He was wrong, totally wrong!

All in all, it takes me almost a year to disentangle myself. But all this happened ten years ago, and I still fantasize about seeing him and telling him that I would never go back with him. Is he like my father? Well, yes, my father was narcissistic and was unable to see me as a separate person. But this man is the Poster Boy for Narcissism. There is a capacity for mild sadism and for contempt that they share. No, we are not talking about S&M. This is all in the emotional realm, a perhaps unconscious predilection for hurting your partner. Was my father seductive? If I were to dig, I would have to say, "maybe."

There's also a longing for symbiosis that binds me. The severing of intense sensual connection felt brutal, whenever we parted. Put more bluntly. getting out of bed was wrenching. Maybe we can blame this part on my mother. There really wasn't anything my therapist could do to help. I was well and truly cooked. One of my friends, who deeply disapproved, said to me, "He is not your friend." Yes, that was true, and I kept repeating to myself, "He is not my friend." That helped a little, I think. Still, there's something to be said for the occasional fantasy.

It's nine years since I finally left him. I still imagine his re-appearance with a thrill of fear and longing.

35. A FRENCH VILLAGE

I dream that Genevieve is moving far away to study theatre. I am weeping, grieving out of all proportion. After all, in real time, both my daughters moved out of New York in the same month, over 20 years ago. Genevieve did tell me on the phone yesterday that neither she nor Julie were going to be able to come to my showcase this time, that she lives faraway. She has, in fact, moved to a new house, even further away.

Both my daughters do come to my semi-annual show regularly and the conversation is unlikely to be the trigger for my dream misery. I had watched a show about the German Occupation of a French village Friday night. I felt spooked in the silent house. Just hearing the curse "les sales boches" made me shudder. The sound of harsh Nazi commands still terrifies me. I only watch one episode and give the rest of the DVDs away to my friend Samuel. Though his parents were both in Auschwitz, he has a stronger stomach for this kind of fare. He lives inside his history. He advises me to watch the whole episode, says it will make me work out some of my demons. I just want to feel better, to stand in the light, to hear music.

I don't know the date of the invasion of Belgium. I look it up. It's May 1940, so I was nearly three years old. I don't remember anything. Everyone must have been scrambling for safety, fearing the worst and it was worse than anyone could have imagined. There must have been panic among all the Jewish refugees, though undoubtedly my parents shielded me as much as possible. There is no way of knowing what I absorbed of their emotional experience. Perhaps it felt safe enough until the convent, that strange, gloomy place, with its long-deserted corridors, the strange women in their unfamiliar black habits. They spoke French, the nuns. I knew only German. My sense of that time is of being surrounded by silence. The only human interaction, I recall, is of a nun slapping me for not eating my gruel.

Lately, I dream of not finding my parents' phone number, not being able to call them or of searching frantically for their address, not being able to visit them. I don't precisely miss them at this time in my life. The dreams are suffused with guilt and anxiety. Yes, I was guilty at five years old, and ever after, perhaps, of not making them happy, of being angry, of not loving them enough. So, I am sad. I feel abandoned this week. I reach out to my daughters. They call me back and it's all better for now.

36. LIFE IN ENGLISH

On my first day of school in the United States, a boy gives me a cartoon book that says "Dick Tracy" on the cover. I am 11-years old, don't speak English, not yet. I am fluent in French and German and have never heard of this "Dick." "Buffalo Bill," who may have been an American, is familiar. We would get stickers with illustrations of his adventures in our Cotes D'Or chocolate bars in Belgium. I would carefully paste them in a book that was to be a story of his life once you collected all the stickers. I do recognize that the boy is offering friendship. This is a class for non-English speaking kids, and everyone seems friendly. The work strikes me as being particularly easy compared to classes in Belgium, where my difficult subjects were sewing, handwriting, and geography. The relationship with the Dick Tracy fan turns out to have very little future. He has the habit of jumping on me from behind which I find alarming. After my complaining to the teacher, he stops, but in retribution for my being a "snitch" he spits at me. Of course, I don't know this expression at the time and have no idea of the dire consequences of "singing" to the authorities.

But on my first day, I like my new dress, navy blue with red polka dots and flounces at the bottom and all seems to be going well. I am puzzled by the recurrent shouts in the classroom of "Mira, Mira." She must be very popular. It isn't till years later that I discover that "Mira" means "look" in Spanish.

We had landed in Hoboken two weeks before. The transatlantic voyage in November took about three weeks and was so stormy that my mother, who was very seasick, stayed in her cabin much of the trip. I sort of enjoyed the swaying of the boat and was intrigued by the dishes sliding off the tables in the dining room. Eating apples took away my nausea. My father went dancing, at every opportunity.

Who says there is nothing to genetic predispositions? There is a photo of me wearing a beanie and a too-tight, too-short brown coat, chubby, but pleased with myself. It is 1948, the year that Truman gets elected President. The headlines in the papers scream "HARRY WINS." My father is shocked. How can you refer to the President as "Harry?"

After the storms and the excitement of the trip, suddenly there is the Statue of Liberty and everyone is standing on deck pointing. We are landing. So here we are in America and whoever told me that everything came in cans here was wrong. There are stalls of fruits and vegetables. But most amazing to me are the huge, brightly lit supermarkets and a novelty gum machine with Juicy Fruit and bubble gum.

Fifty years later my mother will tell me that we waited, sitting on our suitcases, for three hours until someone arrived to greet us. I don't remember this. A politician, Mr. Scheur, had gotten us an affidavit, that is, he sponsored us so we could emigrate. He set us up in an apartment with sky-blue carpets in Manhattan's London

Terrace, an imposing set of buildings on 23rd Street on the West Side. My young mother covered the carpets with newspaper for fear they would get dirty.

One day, for whatever reason, I walk home from school by myself. Naturally I am lost and have to ask directions to 23rd Street. I will soon learn English with the help of Golden Books, but at this point there are few English words in my vocabulary. Eventually I find my way and the doorman, who recognizes me, takes me up to the right apartment. Had I ever been in an elevator? It seems unlikely. No one is home. My mother is probably looking for me at the school, as we routinely walk home together. All of a sudden, I hear the sound of a siren. I panic and wonder if I should be heading to a shelter. Do I realize this is a fire alarm, an ordinary N.Y.C. sound? Probably not until later, when my harried parents arrive to find me safely home.

37. THE MACHETE DANCER

I met Francis when I was still young, if you can call a 70-year-old woman "young." It's all relative, I guess. I had been dancing for two years at that time and wanted a steady dance partner (this was before I met Miguel). I like to dance every dance, preferably with someone who doesn't fling me about, can keep a rhythm and doesn't step on my toes. It's also better if the man doesn't feel the need to teach you the right way to dance, as it's usually the beginners and the guys with two left feet who are driven by the urge to instruct. In theory the leader's job is to make his partner happy and to make her shine, even if she is not a superb dancer. This is very well in theory, but I can't expect to find a partner who even knows this, let alone, can put it into practice. I learn to go with the flow on the turns, so that I don't get my shoulder wrenched out of its socket.

This brings me to the online site, Dance Partners. com. There are plenty of "nonstarters." For instance, there is Leo, the psychiatrist who lives in NYC. We get along famously on the phone. However, when we meet for lunch, it is clear that he doesn't like me. He stares at his plate and is monosyllabic for the 40 excruciating minutes we sit across the table from each other. It turns out, also, that he doesn't know how to dance, isn't particularly interested in dance anyway. Then there is Ramon, a 50-year-old Puerto Rican man who wants a partner to dance club salsa, that is "salsa on two". I tell him that I do "salsa on one," only. This doesn't discourage him. I enjoy talking to him and we send each other emails in Spanish. I like practicing my college Spanish, but I'm suspicious. Why does a good-looking young Latino man need to go online to find a salsa partner? As he isn't giving up, I suggest we meet at a dance. He says, "Oh no, I want you to come to my house on the water in the Bronx." Well, that's the end of that!

Then there is Francis. He is closer to my age and his username is "Electric," which sounds promising. We talk on the phone for about an hour. He tells me he takes salsa lessons with "Fernando." I don't know who that is, but I am impressed. He also tells me he used to be in a Modern Dance Company. I feel that I'm probably not up to his level with my meager two years of private lessons with Alexey. The following week me meet at SOB's, Sounds of Brazil. He tells me he is 6'1 and has long hair. I get lost on the way downtown, keep circling around the block before getting to Varick Street a half hour late. All my energy has gone into getting there and finding a parking space. Here I am, finally, and I see a man who answers to Francis' self-description, standing in the aperture, near the door, beaming at me. His whole being radiates joy. We dance. He throws me around, but I assume it's because I am not a good enough follower. I am somewhat relieved when we adjourn to a nearby diner for what turns out to be a long, congenial conversation. Soon after, we decide to rent studio space weekly in Manhattan and share the cost. I don't remember at what point he starts driving up to my house instead or when he offers to give me a foot massage, or when he starts to spend a day with me every week or when we become lovers. It turns out he is great at massage, though perhaps not great as a dance partner. He prefers doing his own thing too much. That's where Miguel comes in. Alas, I can only speculate about Miguel's talents for massage, but he is a good dance partner. But that comes several years later. Let me tell you more about Francis.

Francis is 72 when we first meet. He is a long-legged hippie who wears his grey hair in a ponytail. The Buddhist sect he belongs to doesn't allow hair cutting, but I know that's just an excuse. Oh yes, he wears earrings—for the same reason. I beg him not to wear the hoops when we are out in public. He also disappears, often in Winter, for occasional week-long retreats, somewhere in the mountains, where there is no heat, no phone and no wi-fi. He wears unfashionable, thick, round glasses. He doesn't wear his hearing aids. Hence the occasional large or minor glitches in communication. His wife (Oh, did I forget to mention he is married?) also doesn't hear very well, especially over the sound of the TV, which reportedly blares all day long. Like any self-respecting hippie he has disdain for soap and water and other niceties, though I never discovered whether the Buddhist sect also prohibits hair washing. This year, he is a dancer. In the years since I have known him, he has been a short story writer, a poet, an actor, a teacher, and a consultant for the arts program at a Nursing Home. He was also an Expressive Arts Therapist for many years. He has been an artist, and has credits in *Who's Who in Art*. Like a tabby cat, he lands in different lives with total aplomb. Sometimes he complains about getting old. He bemoans the fact that he can no longer jump to the height of his head or do a full split. I think, "Why would you want to?" Then I remember that he is a Tae Kwon Do Master, a fifth-degree black belt, taught this discipline for 30 years, and created a Martial Arts Show that toured throughout the country. Oh yes, he also used to walk on machete blades, blindfolded, and was rewarded with much applause.

38. LAST CHA CHA AT THE NURSING HOME

Francis and I are supposed to do a dance show, for a Halloween party, in two months. We did this once before and, at the time, he let me know two days before the performance that he expected me to dance a solo. Just a misunderstanding, it seems. So, there we were at ten p.m., two nights before showtime, bickering on the phone about what music we should use. I say "we," because I insisted that we take turns on stage. He wanted to do something very fast, for Latin shines. Not for me! We compromised on Elvis Presley's "Jailhouse Rock". Miraculously, it went off without a hitch.

But this year we have to plan a dance for a Halloween show, at the Nursing Home where he is consultant. That is, he entertains the residents, dancing for them for hours. His favorite is the Dementia Unit. There he plays with balloons and does pratfalls to the delight of the residents. It is new and wonderful to them every time. We've done shows there before. We have great fun, making up comic scenarios.

During one of our brilliant skits, he was supposed to stab himself with a pencil and stagger into insensibility, all because I rejected his advances. I did my part, playing the diva. I guess he just wasn't upset enough, or I wasn't convincing enough. He stood there on stage looking at me and saying, "What do I do now?" I hissed, "Die, die," and he finally got the message and collapsed on a chair. The audience appeared to be unmoved by any of this. That is, "We died on stage," as they say. They like it better when we choose lively music and get together a reasonably good dance performance. Not easy, as we are pulling in different directions. Francis can do amazing Latin shines. But how long can he keep it up? The audience will be exhausted, just watching, especially as they are mostly wheelchair bound. I wear flashy costumes, say, a hot pink skirt with a bustier and a feather boa and maybe a red feather in my hair, to make up for sketchy choreography. Sometimes the costumes get me through. Sometimes our joint enthusiasm makes up for what we lack in technique.

We are both taking lessons, but not together. We both got frustrated with our joint lessons, not a good omen for partners. We did do several performances at the studio where we take lessons. On one occasion, we wore huge curly wigs and we each had a jumpsuit. Mine was shiny and red and had a halter top and 60s- style bell bottoms. Alexey called it my "drop-dead gorgeous outfit." Francis had a light-blue jumpsuit, very tight. We both wore sunglasses.

Concentrating on the actual routine was challenging as I was overcome by fits of laughter every time, I looked at him. This was our cha-cha-Elvis-Presley moment. Unforgettable! Anyway, we got through the routine to general hilarity on the part of the audience. There had been a buzz, as soon as one of the students caught a glimpse of us at a dress rehearsal. Everyone "had to see this!" It was sort of a "succès de scandal," but most unfortunately, Francis couldn't get out of the costume after the show. There was no dressing room and he was sweating it out in the toilet. Worst of all, from my point of view, he missed my next performance, as he was still trapped in the jump suit in the toilet long after I took my bows. He swore he would never wear that thing again. I expect he threw it in the dustbin. But looking at the photos of us dancing in that getup, afterwards, I do think, we were rather a sight!

So, what do we do for the Nursing Home this year? When Francis heard that it was to be a Halloween party, he said, "I don't want to do it. I'm not going to be a pumpkin or Pinocchio." I convinced him that we could do straight dance in good costumes. We spent a half-hour giggling on the phone about possible personas, for instance Salome and John the Baptist with his head on a tray. I had second thoughts and decided, we better stay away from Biblical characters, in case anyone was religious. The minute we decided to do it, Francis had all kinds of inventive ideas: be a clown, be a slavering dog, be a rattling skeleton, etc. He just can't help himself.

Predictably, the Nursing Home discards the Halloween theme and we are asked to work something up to the music of the eighties. I suggest *Saturday Night Fever* since I had done a showcase dance to the music with Alexey, and I hunt up the old video. Francis doesn't think much of it. He complains that "It's too slow. It's too simple." Simple would be just the thing! However, partners must compromise. Francis makes elaborate charts to write down his various steps. I try to make up a routine. I am enjoying myself and am thinking that maybe I have a knack for choreography. Then I come up against a major problem: Neither one of us is capable of remembering even a third of what I put together, never mind executing it! Time is running short. Over Francis' objections, we turn to Alexey, who puts together a simple routine. Alas, though we can put in our faithful cha-cha routine, the music calls for hustle and Francis has never done the hustle. The week before the fatal performance date, Alexey teaches me to pull and shove Francis into the transitions. As he is over six-feet and I am only five-feet tall and weigh 96 lbs., it isn't pretty when he fights me. There are repetitive arm movements. Alexey stands in front of the studio, waving his arms like an air traffic controller, yelling, "Arms, arms." I am dubious that any amount of rehearsal in the next week will help. Besides, Francis, who lives in Brooklyn, makes it to my neighborhood only once a week.

So, our goose is cooked! Francis' John Travolta suit may not even do the trick!

I get to the Nursing Home early and warm up with staff to the merengue music that relentlessly blasts from the speakers. Francis and his videographer, Benz, get delayed by some subway snafu and are an hour later than agreed. Why am I not surprised that Francis wants even this performance on video? He doesn't want to warm up with me to the salsa music that is now playing. I will make him look bad, as partner dancing cramps his style. The stage, where we were expecting to perform, is crowded with balloons and Halloween decorations. We are relegated to the floor of the Recreation Hall. During the past week, whenever I think of our piece, I remind myself, that the most important thing is to have fun. This good advice is gone the moment the music starts. We are immediately eight counts behind. Never mind, the show must go on. I am grimly counting, pushing and pulling Francis He seems completely lost. I notice there is a man, dancing next to us. Maybe the meager applause at the end of the piece was meant for him. I refuse to watch the video of the evening, and Francis, having seen it, does not insist. The following week, Francis excitedly tells me that the director of the place, who saw us cavorting about, thought we were great. He shook Francis' hand and asked permission to use parts of the video for promotion of their facility. Now, a month later, Francis tells me, that they have cut all funds for Entertainment for the residents. I am heart broken. No more performances for us at the Nursing Home. But there is always the danger that Francis will find another venue!

39. DANCING IN THE CITY

Yesterday, I get into my car to go downtown to dance. It's rainy. It's dark. I say to myself, "If you die in a car crash tonight, you will have had a good life." Later that evening, with merengue music blaring around me, I say to Miguel, "The best part of my life is over." Depressive, all that! I am experiencing a loss. I am feeling my age. Still, Miguel and I we're grooving tonight. I follow effortlessly through tango, cha cha, salsa, fox trot. We even manage some version of the samba. I have stomach cramps, but I am determined to distance from the discomfort, to stay with the music, with the rhythm. Well, my earlier musings are irrelevant of course, just another mood of mine. I want to stay around to dance, to learn a new choreography, to read, to watch movies, and especially to love my daughters. My eulogy would not be all that interesting at this point in my life. Also, I would want a pre-demise party to hear people's testimonials. I have a gorgeous, sequined royal blue dress, which I am saving for my 80th birthday party. I have no other occasion to wear it. I bought it in a fit of enthusiasm from Etsy's, hoping to have it as a dance costume. Natalya tells me that it isn't stretchy enough, so I have to have a party, unless someone has a fancy wedding in the meantime. Here's hoping it will fit me, to sweeten the taste of the end of another decade.

So, what will people say about me? Will friends who don't buy a ticket to watch me dance come to my memorial, or pre-memorial party? Someone will say that I am kind and generous. Whenever I hear that I think, "how boring! My lover has a description of me that I like much better, but it's not suitable for a eulogy and anyway he is now my "ex-lover". I would like to be considered brave, a dancer, intelligent, full of joy, sometimes. Surely, no one will mention the negatives on such an occasion. No one will say that I am lazy, cowardly, people pleasing, self-dramatizing. Damn, why am I always so hard on myself? That goes into the negative column for sure. No one will mention that either and I still have time to reform. My parents lived into their late nineties. But then you never know. There's always that possible crash on the Major Deegan, on a dark rainy night.

40. FRANCIS' WIFE

Yesterday I had a conversation with Francis on speakerphone, so his wife could listen in. At least it isn't covert surveillance. He tells me that "We have a visitor," and that Margaret will be present at our conversation. I say brightly in a way that probably comes across as ironic:

"Really?" Margaret repeats this in a similar tone. We have hit a crisis point. In a moment of exuberance, Francis, one day, last month, thanks Margaret for having been so tolerant of our relationship for the last eight years. It turns out she has misunderstood the situation from the beginning and now she hates me and now she is threatening divorce, unless Francis and I sever all connections. This phone call situation smacks of the prisoner's last permitted call before the beginning of his sentence. Still, I am rather glad to be able to say in Margaret's hearing that I am sorry about the misunderstandings that have brought suffering to all of us. I am not too bothered by Margaret's listening in and am glad to be able to tell Francis the news of the week. After all, it is not the Stasi and I have been duly warned to avoid any indiscretions. Our conversation is boring enough that she dozes off somewhere in the middle of the news in review.

There aren't many more conversations after this one. Francis, who abides by his promises, agrees to sever all contact with me. I have saved his last passionate love letter to me, but shortly thereafter, all that remains are memories and a deafening silence.

41. TALES OF THE TANGO CITY

I am going by train. There is no parking in midtown in the afternoon. I decide to wear my fleece pants, an L.L. Bean cotton turtleneck, and my fuzzy lavender fleece. Very unsexy. The idea is to change into pantyhose and a skirt when I get there. I hesitate over the choice of black skirt. One is too short in case I decide to keep on my thigh-high black spandex socks, another tends to slide down, as it's too loose. The third one is just out of the machine and is miraculously dry. It goes into my backpack, along with my black, sensible practice shoes and my gold ballroom shoes. The gold shoes are the only ones I can wear right now, and I bring them in case I stay for the Saturday night milonga. I also put in the backpack a peanut butter sandwich, oatmeal cookies, and fruit for Miguel, half a sandwich for me, a bottle of water, a paperback copy of Armistead Maupin's *Tales of the City* to read on the train, my wallet with money to pay Miguel and for my train fare, and a few dollars in case of adventure. I also pack a small case with cosmetics, which I know I won't use, dental floss, painkillers and of course my mints. I'm making progress in getting out the door. But first I have to prepare my feet. I tie down my hammer toe, I apply pain patches to the ball of my foot and apply bunion pads. Finally, I put on my long L.L. Bean coat. The hood doesn't allow for peripheral vision, but it's cold. I will have to be cautious. I get on my clumsy, somewhat waterproof boots and get into my dented 11-year-old green Toyota. I recognize it from a distance, by its only having one hub cap. There is ample parking by the train today, as most sensible people stay, cozy and warm, at home in a snowstorm. I am comfortable on the train, curled up in my coat, reading my novel. Across from me, a woman flashes me a warm smile. I feel somehow welcomed. Grand Central comes all too soon. I search for my MetroCard, check that my gloves, with their hand warmers, are still in my pocket. As I make my way down the stairs to the shuttle, I hear someone playing music, seemingly oblivious to the cacophony of arriving and departing trains. It's rush hour and everyone is pushed along by the crush of bodies. On the shuttle, a burly man rocks a tiny baby, curled up in a pouch on his chest. He talks to it softly. The baby's mother adjusts a little white sock that is sliding off his foot. I'm thinking the tiny foot must be cold. The woman, sitting next to me, beams and says in awe, "It's a newborn." We both smile. The little one! The subway is a rough baptism, but the baby is wrapped in a protective cocoon.

When I get out to Times Square, it is still snowing. I drag myself the seven slushy blocks to the studio. It's wet and slippery. I feel about one-hundred years old. You walk into the largest space in the studio to get to the dressing room. It smells of sweat. Scantily dressed dancers, all in black, are gyrating on the floor. There are three separate lessons going on. One of the dancers is practicing samba walks, moving incrementally in a grinding rotation of the hip. A couple whizzes along the floor, spinning into a dance of seduction. There is also a student being taught the rudiments of cha cha, the instructor, turning her body into the proper form. I track in with my wet boots, taking care to stay out of the path of hurtling bodies. It's packed in the dressing room tonight. I see that Maria is there. She is a recent widow, who has fallen in love with the tango. Nothing disturbs her equanimity. Everything is always perfect. That begins to irritate me, big time. Tall Renate is changing into a clingy top and putting on makeup. She is evidentially planning on staying for the milonga, which is due to start about two hours after our workshops. She never says a word but smiles once in a while. I hang up my coat and my damp socks, slip out of my boots and make my way to the toilet to change into panty hose and skirt. I put on my black practice shoes. I am still frumpy. Emil is late, but we use the private studio to warm up. Maria and Renate practice tango walks. I warm up with stretches, lunges and leg swings. Oscar has called to say he will be late. Morris, a guy with a huge belly and a homely face, arrives with Oscar right behind him. Emil finally arrives, 20 minutes late. He is laden down with bottles of soda, chips, napkins etc. for the milonga. Miguel is still not there. He's usually punctual and it's not like him not to call. Did he have an accident, riding his bicycle on the slushy road, dodging impatient drivers. Maybe he went to the wrong studio. There might be a sensible explanation, but for me, there is always a catastrophe waiting to happen. In the meantime, a woman in stiletto heels joins the group. She is tall with very black hair, black leggings and sunglasses. She smiles at me pleasantly, but that should have been Miguel walking in the door, not this siren. This is one of those days when I consider whether I would persist with tango if it weren't for Miguel. It makes me sad to think that I have gotten so dependent on him these last two years. He arrives with 15 minutes left to the first workshop, but he hasn't missed much. It is a Stage Tango class and we keep on repeating the same maneuver. Emil keeps saying, "It's wrong. It's totally wrong." We don't get anywhere. Then it's time for the Milonga Workshop, which is to lead to a group performance. Morris and the woman in stilettos; Renate and Maria are passed around between Oscar and Emil. I get to keep Miguel to myself. The piece is to start with the woman doing a rapid spin and falling into a dip on her partner's arm. For some reason, I am worried about my back and my toe hurts, and my arthritic knee is grinding audibly. Miguel and I decide I will lift my arm for the spin, so it can land, gracefully, on his shoulder. I try this with Emil and hit him in the face. No, that won't do! For the dip, Miguel tells me to keep my head in line with my torso. Emil says to let my head hang down. The rest of the choreography proceeds, pretty smoothly. We know it will change, as Emil won't remember any of it and, unless we film, it's all gone. I limp out to change, feeling demoralized. Maria is cheerfully putting on makeup for the milonga. Sadly, I am preparing to make my way back to the shuttle, to the commuter train, and home. Miguel says, "Let's go get some coffee and talk a bit." Suddenly the spring is back in my step. We walk the long block to the dumpy diner, where we often hang out before the Saturday night milonga. It's out of the way, but I no longer feel pain and it doesn't matter. As usual, I order decaf tea. You can't go too far wrong with that.

He has coffee and we order a side of sweet potato fries to share. My misery dissipates, as if, by magic. He is in a good mood and tells me about a visit from his son. I will be late for the ten-p.m. train, but never mind. On the shuttle platform there's a band playing Beatles' songs. And then I hear the Rolling Stones' "I can't get no satisfaction." I am singing along, and the crowd is rocking. Young and old, stylish and shabby, we are having a party in this dark, cavernous space. We're tapping our feet, moving our bodies, clapping to the music. The shuttle comes all too soon, but I have my book and will soon be reading on the train, on the way home.

42. SURGERY

Finally, this Summer, my troublesome hammer toe is to be amputated. Ouch! It sounds better when you say "disarticulated." I have been postponing this surgery for several years now. Has it been two years, three years? I get lost in time. It all merges into just yesterday. The severely dislocated toe makes it impossible for me to wear most shoes, but there is always another choreography to learn, another showcase, and I keep deciding that I can manage a little longer. The doctor reassures me that it will be quick and dirty, with two weeks recovery time

But I manage a long time without the surgery. In warm weather, I can wear Munro sandals, much the worse for unexpected rain damages. For the Winter there's a pair of oversized, much battered UGGs. Alexey tells me cheerfully that Stalin had a hole in his boot to accommodate just such an unruly toe. I do have a hole in my boot, but it's on the wrong foot and serves no purpose except to make me feel exceedingly shabby. For dance, I have a pair of practice shoes with old lady stacked heels. I can adjust the laces so that my toe can stick out on top. I have a pair of peeling gold dance shoes that I can wear, after stretching the left one for several weeks. Natalya, who orders the shoes for me (she orders several pairs at a time, because they wear out quickly) tells me they have stopped making this particular model. I spend hours at a dance shoe store hoping to find a shoe that will accommodate my toe, my aching metatarsals and my bunion. No luck! It is all most unglamorous, not to mention, regrettable.

It is time to deal with the situation, but will I be able to dance after keeping my foot elevated for two weeks? I can't look at that question too directly at this time.

I decide to tell Alexey that under the circumstances, I shouldn't learn a new dance. It would be fine to just repeat the Pit Bull piece and the newly refurbished "Newfangled Tango" that I did four years ago. He nods, but since the new dance is already partly choreographed, he teaches it to me and has me repeat it every lesson. The deadline for learning it is my surgery date. You don't argue with Alexey! Besides, I really want to do it. But, a week before the surgery, I have an arthritic flare up in my right knee and it's the left toe that is to go. How will I manage crutches? I am walking through rehearsals and slavering anti-inflammatory gel on my knee, on my toes and on my metatarsal.

I am to dance with Miguel this Sunday. I know, I know I shouldn't go, but I really want to and who knows when I will get to dance again. I feel anxious and emotional on the trip downtown. I wear a long dress to hide my knee brace. I hope I can get on my shoes, as the toe seems to have gotten worse, re-enforcing my decision to get rid of the pesky thing. Miguel is a bit late and I am dying to dance the first rumba and the fox trot that follows. We dance. I hurt, but I tell myself I can rest after the surgery, won't need to be hopping around on that leg right away. I don't do the Viennese waltz and I probably should have skipped the samba, but I am happy. Somehow, I will get through the last week's rehearsal.

When we leave, we see it's snowing a bit, but it doesn't feel as cold as earlier. I still feel the glow of the evening, as I drive down 34th Street to the West Side Highway. There isn't even any traffic. There will be surgery soon and maybe some discomfort, but I want to stay grateful for tonight, even as I soak my feet in cold water when I get home.

43. MORE ABOUT MIGUEL

When we first met four years ago at Emil's Stage Tango Group, we had a flirty dalliance, kissing and holding hands. At rehearsals for our first show together, we would giggle in corners, excited and happy around each other, trying out sexy moves. But I didn't accept any of his invitations to go to his apartment. I sensed that he was too likely to distance. Already I wanted to talk to him, write to him, touch him all the time. Also, of course, there was Francis to consider. In truth, if it hadn't been for Francis, I would have gone for it and damn the consequences.

Now we are friends and we dance together. He is a professional dancer, neat, trim, courteous to a fault. Tonight, we sit and talk for a while, before dancing. He is in general somewhat aloof, so that I am pleased when he says: "I thought of calling you to ask you to come earlier, so we could talk a bit." Our first dance is a slow rumba and I have trouble hearing the rhythm and getting my balance. We move into cha cha, salsa, swing. I follow the sinuous movement of his hips. Another rumba, he holds me close. In tango we do leg wraps and I feel his leg lingering next to mine. I am laughing, moving comfortably in tune with him. Sometimes when we dance, I feel that I am the happiest woman in the room.

When all this started, I said to myself, "Do you have to have every sweet plum that comes your way?" I felt, "Yes, oh yes." My sensible brain said, "No."

44. GETTING THROUGH THE NIGHT

I wake at four a.m. My body feels rigid. I must get out of bed. I must wake up. It's night and we are being hunted down. We pack some essentials. We need to escape. We are going to be set on fire. I try to go back to sleep, but I can't escape my nightmarish fate.

I must think of something else. I take some Tylenol, eat some crackers and half a banana. I would turn on my fail-safe middle of the night music, Chopin Nocturnes, but the boom box is disconnected. Why not think of last night on the dance floor with Miguel? But it doesn't seem to matter what happens in my waking life. Dreams have a life of their own. They are usually dark, often frightening.

Okay, okay, last night! I wasn't feeling that well and almost didn't go. When I got to Starlight Ballroom, Miguel, to my amazement says: "You may not feel so well, but you look marvelous. Have I seen that dress before?" He must be in a good mood. He never says things like that to me. He smiles more than usual. We touch more as we dance. Has anything changed?

45. SUNDAY AFTERNOON

It used to be called Jude's Dancing Studio after Jim Jude, the guy who ran the place, the guy who paid the bills, hired and fired teachers. He was a sullen host and teacher with a somewhat unsavory reputation, but the socials were well attended. Anyway, as several people told me, there was a scandal that brought about the collapse of Jude's. Perhaps, it's best to draw a curtain around the much bruited about details, that were perhaps more or less true.

The studio has been under new ownership for several years now. In any case someone else runs the operation. This past Sunday was sort of a homecoming for me, as I hadn't been there for many years, preferring to drive downtown to dance with Miguel. Despite the time away, everything felt so familiar. It looks the same. There still is the struggle up a long winding staircase. I remember once seeing one of the dancers climb up on all fours, to then happily cha cha the night away. The toilets are still downstairs. The acoustics are deplorable. It takes a while to identify the music coming out of the muted loudspeakers. Still, the busy Wednesday nights were fun and exciting, some of the time. It's comforting to be back in a familiar place. Unpleasant memories flash briefly through my mind. Today there are no worries about having to sit out too many dances or of being annoyed by men, who know you for years, but won't make eye contact, for fear you'll get the idea that they would deign to dance with you that evening.

There were also the willing but clumsy dancers, who felt it their mission to teach you and those who pulled and pushed you, in an effort to assert their manhood.

Today Dora and I are dancing with Alexey. He wants us to practice our routines. That unnerves me a bit. Everything unnerves me these days. So much for the wisdom of age, so much for studies that say the elderly are happier because they no longer have to accomplish anything or prove anything to themselves and others. In the event, as they play odd music like the polka, there is little opportunity to show off my samba routine. We do enough free style ballroom dancing to please me, to make me feel free and happy for a while. Being "in the zone" is hard won, comes seldom and almost never when doing a choreographed routine.

If I were to make a new year's resolution, it would be "Be grateful." The moments of realizing you are blessed don't come easily either. But, if you were to ask me, "do you wish, you were young again?" my unequivocal answer would be "no." Accepting aging with equanimity still eludes me. I am often lonely, at a loss, disappointed in myself, but there is freedom, these moments of grace on the dance floor, the excitement of learning, my growing curiosity about the world. Arthritis and wrinkles be damned!

46. SHOES

It's raining again on this my second trip this month to Worldtone, the Mecca for dance shoes in Manhattan. My feet usually hurt by the time I get there. These are occasions of discomforting anxiety. Also, there are vague feelings of shame. It's irrational. It's nonsense. Why should there be all this emotion, not to mention rain, attached to buying a pair of dance shoes. The store is on Eighth Avenue, between 38th & 39th Streets. Hordes of people jostle me on the sidewalk. There are several fast-food joints on every block: Pizza, Mexican, Arby's. None of them sound remotely appealing. Anyway, there's the important mission of buying shoes for the next Showcase.

Nothing ever fits and most everything hurts. That's perhaps an exaggeration, but no, not really. The shoe should have a heel (a 2-inch heel will do) and be beige or tan, preferably satin. For tango, my teacher tells me that most of the "girls" now wear 3 1/2 or 4-inch heels. At the milongas, you can see women leaning into their partners, sometimes towering over them, in their pretty, for me impossible shoes.

I do own a pair of what I think of as "old lady shoes" in black with a stacked 1 1/2-inch heel, which I happily wear to go dancing, while still ogling other women's more exciting footwear. My old 2-inch heels hurt me, and I have to steel myself to start wearing them at least one month before the show to practice. Alexey tells me that the old lady shoes in tan would be fine with the right color Capezio mesh stockings to match, so that there would an uninterrupted line of the leg. But they are ugly! But they are comfortable! On the first of my two rainy trips, I also bring home a pair of delicious satin Supadance shoes with a 2-inch heel, just to try out. They are o.k. in the store of course, though the heel is thin and promises a balance challenge. Do I give in to being an old lady? The "Desiderata" poster in my kitchen advises: "Relinquish gladly the things of youth." Yes, but those shoes are so pretty! On yesterday's trip Miguel sways, me, saying: "It's the dance that counts. You should have comfortable shoes." He had agreed to meet me there, making the trip a less negative experience. He immediately finds a pair that fit him perfectly, on sale even. Oh, my ugly new and expensive shoes!

47. HEARTBREAK, JEALOUSY, AND BLOOD ON THE FLOOR

Emil and I are rehearsing for our tango performance. Miguel calls it a "Demonstration," which sounds less grandiose, more appropriate. I like that better. We rehearse for about six weeks, but Emil keeps forgetting the routine. I don't remember the sequence myself, as it keeps changing. Emil, who has the reputation of being "a drama queen," likes to give impassioned, soulful looks to his partners when he performs. I try to control my impulse to giggle, but he sees my lips trembling with the effort and loses the thread. It is meant to be theatre, of course, but it's not always easy to get in character as a smoldering tango dancer, trembling with passion. You are not supposed to take tango lightly. The music is all about heartbreak, jealousy, and blood on the floor.

But we are doing tango vals. We glide, we spin. I feel light and free with vals. Emil often dances one with me at the end of a lesson, because it makes me happy, and of course also because he wants me to come back for another expensive lesson. On his better days, Emil amuses me with his antics. I smile throughout the "Demonstration," and no one calls me heartless for not weeping along with the music, in this case "Desde el alma," meaning "from the soul." Another couple dances that afternoon. Their music keeps resonating in my mind. It's called in Spanish "Olvidame," but the translation is "Remembrance." When I tell Emil that I like this music, he picks up on the cue, without missing a beat. He says, "It's very romantic. I could do a nice choreography for you. I will make it hard, because you are a dancer. I always like to make it harder for you. The other couples' dance was easy." Then he dances the song with me, miming romance and passion. Hmm, really lovely! I remind myself that it's expensive, that it's exhausting to keep trekking into the city, to prepare for a two-minute dance and that, yes, that for all his entertainment value, Emil can be exasperating. He begins campaigning for me to do another performance three weeks into the rehearsal for this one. Now his efforts are escalating. "You were amazing," he says at the end of the evening.

Emil seems genuinely excited that he was able to repeatedly spin me in a *gancho*, with both of us extending one free arm, wowing the audience. He tells me of people's excitement about my high lift. I finally learned to keep my body upright, reaching for the ceiling and he does six full turns. At one of our early rehearsals, I leaned back and both of us crashed to the floor. He sustained mild injuries and I was embarrassed. Anyway, you had to see the more polished version. Lots of applause!! People love these showy tricks. We even finish the dance on time to the music. It takes some improvisation on his part, but not as much as I had feared.

I am leaving out the brouhaha about the dress. I have one sexy tango dress. Sometimes the costume compensates for a less than smooth execution. When I wear it to a rehearsal, it snags on his buttons, on the glide down from the lift. So, it was back to the closet for something appropriate, but in the event rather dull. I suppose the lift made up for it!

48. DON'T QUIT YOUR DAY JOB?

When I get to 36th Street, I spot an ample parking space, right across the street from the studio. Alas, I end up on the sidewalk. I am a mediocre driver at best, partly because of being massively spatially impaired. I know it's going to be a struggle to right this situation. I notice a man on the other side of the street eying me warily, as I turn the wheel this way and that. I get out to see how I am doing and throw my coat off. How come it's so much warmer in Manhattan than upstate? I wonder what people might think about a little old lady in a flouncy, very short dress.

When, with the car finally parked, I get to the ballroom, I tell Miguel about my embarrassing experience. He says, "You should have opened your window and called out, 'Hey, I charge admission'." Slowly people drift in. I don't know most of their names, but it's comforting to see familiar faces. One of the regulars sits slumped in a chair, looking glum. I know that he is transformed when the music starts and he hits the dance floor. In fact, I can't help laughing at his antics. He does some version of the hokey pokey with a more or less cooperative partner. He seems to be having a blast. Miguel tells me that he has been doing the same routine for 20 years. "O.K., but it's still funny." I wonder if his partner must be getting frustrated and may wish to dance, say, a traditional cha cha. Miguel says, "Don't worry, she is being well paid." This guy's very young partner (she could not be much more than 20 years old) looks very bored and keeps checking her cell phone when they sit out a dance. He dances with an older woman for a few dances and she enthusiastically plays along with him. Of course, old men must have very young girls by their side. But sometimes it cuts the other way as well. I see Miriam, in an elegant, navy-blue sequined gown, come in with her current partner. She is almost 90 years old and I hear she has been dancing for ten years. Her partner, an attentive, well-dressed young man in his 30s, leads her with care and seeming affection. I know that she is a Holocaust survivor, as there has been an announcement about a film about her experiences that won a prize at Cannes. She invites Miguel to see the film, but never makes eye contact with me. She is still beautiful, with a vivid face and an elegant figure, which is marred only by a stooped shoulder, caused no doubt by osteoporosis. I guess she is the type of woman, much admired by men in her youth, who never had any use for other women. Miriam's former partner, Tony, also very young, was very friendly and always greeted both of us effusively. We wondered whether he and Miriam had a falling out, as these days he appears with a younger woman. Her name is Ella, my grandmother's name, so that I have no difficulty remembering it. She remembers "Miguel," but whenever I see her, she says, with a question mark in her voice, "Nancy? Norah?" Anyway, we get re-acquainted in short order, hug and kiss on both cheeks like old friends. I am intrigued when Tony says that he is the first man she has danced with, as she comes from an orthodox Jewish background. Now I wish we could wrangle a coffee date with them, so I could find out more.

It is always amazing to find out what people do off the dance floor. The man with two left feet is a neurosurgeon with a thriving practice. The smoothest dancer in the room is a guard at Rikers Island. I wonder what the skinny bent-over man with a ponytail, who asks me to dance when Miguel goes to get some food, does for a living. He approaches me the first time, saying, "I know you are a professional." I am flattered, but demur. He is a terrible dancer (so not a dancer), with no sense of rhythm and the merengue seems endless. Now I avert my face if I see him heading in my direction. In tango, you lock eyes to seal the promise that you're are going to share the next dance. Of course, since it's ballroom, he could simply tap me on the shoulder. I know this is mean. I have been in his position. In the past, too many men have avoided looking at me, or saying hello, for fear they might be trapped into dancing with me. O.k., I am human. He does ask me one more time. It's really too mean to say "no," and this time it is not so bad.

There is Darren, who told me he works with stained glass and used to be a dancer at the Joffrey Ballet. Who knows? It's possible. I haven't seen him in a long time. He is possibly my age. He always wears a hat and is at least semi-intoxicated. I met him at one of my first milongas. He rescued me from having to sit out the evening. He kept me laughing, testing my flexibility and endurance with various wild dips and drops.

I don't see Belle, tonight. I know her also from tango. She is a woman in her 80s who wears even more extravagant gowns than Miriam. She has expensive, stylish jewelry and owns several wigs. She is a good tango dancer. I am not sure with whom she dances these days, but they are always young. She has her own interior design business and a number of employees, who, no doubt, snap to when she gives an order. She tells me that she was married for three months, when she told her husband to go back to his mother. I imagine that for her men are a convenience to be used and discarded at will.

49. WALLFLOWER

They played a lot of hits from the fifties tonight at the dance social. I was a teenager in that era, an oddball always carrying a thick novel under my arm. I was clueless about popular culture, a girl without any prospect of a boyfriend. I was a wallflower in Junior High School and it rarely even entered my mind to go to any High School dances. At home, the radio dial was set at WQXR. Did I even know how to turn the knob and change the station? Did I dare? It didn't occur to me. I didn't know anything about the latest music. I danced around the living room to tunes from *The Nutcracker Suite*, especially "The Waltz of the Flowers".

There were some, perhaps more tuned in, friends in school and in the neighborhood, in Washington Heights. We used to sit on the Wall overlooking the Hudson River. A guy, called Joe Costello, once explained to me how I should defend myself: Go for the eyes with your fingers, then kick...well you know the rest. My school, The Bronx High School of Science, was geographically inconvenient. I had few friends in school and didn't participate in after-school activities. One of my classmates, Ethelbert, who lived near me, chided me for keeping low, i.e., not good enough company. On the other hand, he made no attempt to befriend me. I looked him up recently. He has prestigious friends, is an important person. Well, with a name like his, you have to overcompensate. A kinder way to put it would be that "he had to live up to his name." Morris, another of the local boys who went to Science was content to be my friend. I used to call him "my little brother." When we met up fifty years later, he told me that he and his entire family were convinced we were going to get married. I did have a boyfriend—though not Morris!—for about two months when I was sixteen. He wore his hair slicked back into a kind of pompadour. He wore his jeans slung low with a garrison belt and a brown leather jacket. A large cross dangled from his neck. He was super cool looking in a *West Side Story* kind of way. They called it looking "rocky" then. He was known as Rex, but he told me his Greek name, which I remember more or less accurately to this day: "Vassil Demetrius Zacharoyana." In my yearbook, he declared that I was to be his future wife. Ethelbert most definitely disapproved.

I also had a friend named Meg, whose real name was Julie, and there was Jennifer, who was pretty with her black curly hair and rosy cheeks. I heard later that eventually she married a man who gambled away a fortune. There was also Mary-Ann, a skinny girl with a pixie cut, who wore jeans and slouched a bit. She had what they used to call "a reputation." The gossip was that she had slept with several boys in the neighborhood and there was talk of shunning her. We hardly knew each other in the first place, but when I told my mother this story, she encouraged me to befriend her, if anything. I never found out more about Mary-Ann or about the stories that were circulating. It all was a bit tantalizing, exciting perhaps. At sixteen years old, all my information about life came from Dostoevsky novels, except for that kiss with Rex by the elevator in my apartment building. Mostly that felt awkward as we bumped noses. After this unromantic kiss, there was some necking in the movie theatre, during a cast of thousands production of *The Ten Commandments*. It was probably just as well that we didn't see any of the movie during these sessions. Anyway, the romance with Rex didn't last, in spite of his promise that he would be my future husband. After two and a half months, he started to date my best friend Delia, though I don't think he promised to marry her too. I must look like the marrying type. Even now, when I happen to be standing near a man, any man at all, tall, fat, short, handsome, young or old, people assume he is my husband. That we would be strange bedfellows doesn't deter people from jumping to conclusions.

I did eventually get to hear popular music. Our neighborhood gang found a room in a local building on Riverside Drive, which we called our clubhouse. We would dance there, moving very close together. I didn't know how to do the lindy, but one of the guys tactfully said that I was too graceful for that dance. I remember that the music aroused all kinds of longing in me. Hearing it tonight made me remember how I so much wanted to be held and to dance as a young girl. Tonight's music pulls me back into a time of painful unfulfilled adolescent fantasies. How liberating to be eighty years old and dancing to my heart's content.

50. ANCESTRY

I record that I was born in Königsberg, East Prussia in 1937, at the dawn of the Nazi Era. Königsberg has become Kalingrad in Poland but that doesn't change the circumstances of my birth. What if it were possible to start over, to dream up a different beginning in a sunny climate, somewhere on the Mediterranean? Perhaps *Ancestry DNA* could give clues to my longing for warmth and color, for the vibrancy of a non-Teutonic culture. There must be an explanation for my gravitating to everything Latin, for my repeated attempts to learn Spanish, for my lifelong attachment to my now probably deceased first love, Joe Pacheco.

Starting over, of course, is not an option, except in fantasy. It's regrettable that writing fiction is out of my comfort zone, probably because of want of imagination. Instead, I have lived through other writers' novels, starting with *Little Women*, all the way to what seizes my fancy these days. As I reflect, it emerges that my favorite reading has been Thomas Mann, Tolstoy, Dostoevsky, Chekhov. These are not authors from sunny climes, full of laughter and sensuality. And then there are the treasure troves of the English: Dickens, Trollope, of course Shakespeare, and these days almost any British woman writer. And England, well it's raw. It rains a lot in the Winter and there's poor central heating. It's way too chilly and what about that "stiff upper lip?" All that politeness and restraint? Perhaps there is no escaping my heritage. Perhaps I am not meant to frolic in the ocean and make love on the beach.

Still there is Latin music and dance, the mellifluous sound of Spanish and Italian and of course, the men! Perhaps, you can be Teutonic and Italian or from worlds still unknown, all at the same time. There is no escaping from darkness and confusion in any culture. But I can go to the beach, even fully clothed, and I can read anything translated into English, and I can also read French novels and laboriously, nowadays, some Spanish too.

51. DREAMING OF FRANCIS

I'm eating my oatmeal when the phone rings. I am also reading the last two pages of a thrilling mystery. I don't like being interrupted, but it could be important. You never know. It's Francis on the line. He says, "Hi, love, I will be there at one o'clock, as usual." Wait a minute! What is happening here? It is a year and a half, more or less, since Francis' wife has ordered him to cut off all contact with me. There were to be no phone calls, no emails and certainly no visits, under threat of making his life utterly miserable if he didn't comply. He keeps his word and there has been no word from him. So, what has suddenly changed? Did he mislay our too-long separation in some cut-off compartment of his mind? He tends to be forgetful. That probably hasn't gotten better since we last talked. He was able to retrieve my phone number and that's a good sign.

But how can he be calling me out of the blue, as though nothing had happened? I know I didn't hallucinate our painful parting. Well, I think, you must not look a gift horse in the mouth or is this a Trojan horse and I should beware of Greeks bearing gifts? I know the Trojans have nothing to do with the case, but I like "Timeo Danaos et dona ferentes," as my ex-husband often quoted. We were in Latin class together at City College and he did call me unexpectedly after our separation, though I rejected the olive branch. But I do digress, and I am certainly mixing my myths and metaphors.

Rather than be silent, I say, "Sure, I will pick you up at the train." Do I have time to take a shower and put on some more fetching clothes? Of course, he never notices what I am wearing anyway. I do make a stab at clarifying the situation and say, "Isn't there something you wanted to tell me?" He says, "I was going to tell you when I got there. There's a lot of interest in my book and I have picked up another 500 followers on Facebook. I am bringing you my next two chapters. I hope you won't mind going over them. Something isn't working in the second chapter." This does sound like the Francis I know. It is definitely not an imposter. I am flummoxed. His book has been published and is being sold on Amazon. I didn't buy it, partly because I am angry at him for just writing me off and also because I am not so impressed with his writing or with my own revisions for that matter. Also, I don't get why his story of his trip to Thailand is so fascinating. He was adding some cartoons when I last saw the manuscript and I *was* looking forward to seeing those.

But here we are in some kind of circular time warp. That was two Summers ago. Which show dances was I working on at that time? It might have been the drum piece in the purple bodysuit. I still had five toes then on my left foot. An extreme hammer toe was amputated this past October. I look down at my feet. Yes, there are now four toes, which means I can wear shoes other than sandals and my oversized Uggs. It was Francis who first suggested amputation. I first thought he was crazy, as he is mostly very eccentric, and it sounded like a scary prospect. Has he aged in the past year? He doesn't or didn't have any lines on his face and had a good strong body. He just didn't hear well and would guess at what I might be saying, often getting it wrong in hilarious ways. He also routinely forgot what I had told him, even if he did hear it. I am a "space cadet," but he exists way in outer space. More likely, we both live inside our own heads, more or less of the time. Has any of this changed, has it gotten worse? Part of him, perhaps, has been frozen in time, in the routine of getting together every Tuesday, his taking the subway in

Brooklyn and the train from Grand Central to Hartsdale. In those days he would get immersed in a group playing music at the train station and would dance to entertain whatever audience materialized. He loved an audience, lived for applause. He told me that the caption in his HS Yearbook read: "He will yet be famous!" He would arrive on time without fail, in spite of distractions. We would happily make love, talk, laugh, listen to music and dance. We would both be high on love as we shared a simple supper before I drove him back to the train, also on time.

He seems to have forgotten that things went haywire after, in a moment of elation, he thanked his wife for having been so accepting of our affair the last eight years. Her hearing and memory are no better than his and who knows what she had been thinking, forgetting, remembering. In any case it was all over and as one of my friends imagines it, he is now chained up in the basement of the marital house.

In any case, Francis had to stop dancing, too, sometime before our enforced separation. He had some kind of dangerous vascular problem. I sometimes look at his Facebook page. I see that he writes, "I used to be a dancer. Now I am a writer." So, he does have a notion of past tense. He is or was a Buddhist and the aim, I understand, is to exist only in the present. But what is the present without the past? The past is still with me, no matter how much I meditate.

Let's be honest: I don't meditate at all and the last time that Francis called was more than a year and a half ago.

52. DINNER WITH MIGUEL

It's Christmas season. Every year, since I have known him, Miguel flies to California to see his family. It is also his birthday. He tells, with a hint of excitement, that he will be in NYC for his birthday for the first time in many years. On impulse I tell him that I want to take him out to dinner to celebrate. Some part of me yearns to spoil him, to give him gifts. Many times, I restrain myself, don't let him guess at my affection for him. I don't want to embarrass him. He somewhat reluctantly agrees to let me treat him to a meal at a posh restaurant. He says, "We could just go to our diner and have sweet potato fries." I veto that idea. The diner is a dingy, dirty midtown establishment. It just happens to be close to the Saturday night milonga and a handy place to chat a little before dancing. Joe Allen's, where we decide to go, is in the Theatre District and Miguel reminds me that it is pricey. Maybe, we shouldn't do it, he says. In reality, I too, feel awkward about the plan. I feel that I don't belong in an upscale restaurant. What shall I wear? My boots are shabby. I brush my wool coat. It has seen ten years of wear and I still like it, but is it presentable? My first association to this outing is of "the Little Match Girl." What is that about? I own a house in the suburbs. It may not be in prime condition, but I am hardly homeless. Still, I am that little girl, her nose pressed up against the bakery window. I remember that, during the war, my parents used to send me to the bakery for bread. I was three years old and cute. How could they refuse? I think that my odd reaction has something to do with still being in hiding.

On the appointed day, I take the earlier of two possible trains into Grand Central. I made a reservation. It wouldn't do to be late. I shuttle across to Times Square. Of course, I have about 40 minutes to kill. It would be gauche to get there so early. As it turns out, there's a singer in the station with a powerful Aretha Franklin type of voice, entertaining an enthusiastic group of people. Men, women, and teens are singing along and moving to the music. She sings Michael Jackson's "Billy Jean." A young woman is doing "moonwalks" and is gesturing with verve, if maybe not with musicality. I am restrained from cutting loose by my bulky coat and the aforementioned shabby boots. Also, I am too embarrassed to make a spectacle of myself, even if it's in front of strangers I will never see again. The singer approaches various people with her mike, inviting them to sing along. There's a tiny, old woman, all bent over and wearing heavy purple eyeliner, standing next to me. She gamely joins the chorus. I step back, hiding a little. Then suddenly it's over. It's her last song, before joining her family for dinner, she says. The crowd disperses and I head out into the wintery streets, dragging my feet, in spite of the bitter cold. I can't be that early? It's a trip to see all the lit-up theatres, where I also feel I don't belong. What's up with that? But I can enjoy the glitz. I step into a Duane Reade to warm up, but it's not too interesting. Interesting and safely invisible are contradictory experiences. I do know that, in theory, anyway. I soldier on, past other establishments some, rather seedy. As I get to 8th Avenue, I pass a place, called "The Gentleman's Club." This time it is my common sense that tells me, that I don't belong there. The big guys guarding the place look like TV type thugs. I rush by, walking in the road, avoiding the too crowded sidewalk. Too much testosterone in the atmosphere! Yes, interesting and safe are contradictory experiences.

I find the restaurant easily and am just five minutes early. The hostess makes no comment about my punctuality. She is friendly and shows me to a corner table. The room is lovely, with small candles on every table. It's both elegant and romantic. Miguel arrives soon after. He is always handsome, never out of place, though he tells me that he probably hasn't spent more than $200 on clothes, his entire life. He's still worried about the cost of the evening, but I instruct him to not look at the prices. It really is much nicer than the diner. It feels a little like a dream. We are elegant people, in some movie. I could learn to live like that!

53. SUMMER DOLDRUMS

They tell you to be mindful, the Zen people, mindful of how you feel emotionally and physically. I am not sure that is a great idea. At least today it feels like a dubious solution. Yesterday I closed my eyes, was still, felt my eyes filling with tears, about what? Mortality maybe? being lonely? missing my lover?

This morning my head hurts. I woke out of a panicky dream of messing up, of calling for my daughters, who had disappeared. Long holiday weekends in Summer, I feel apart from others. I should be enjoying the balmy days, but am holed up at home, alone. Where is everyone? Alexey is on vacation and I am not in the mood for his favorite merengue cure. I can't write myself out of this funk. Maybe the library is open for a few more hours!

54. TIME

Yesterday at the milonga, I ask Miguel: "Are you really okay?" He is retreating into himself, into his small apartment. I am sitting in my car, when I see him arriving on his bicycle. He looks glum, has dark rings under his eyes. He says, "I feel that I am running out of time." I wish I had asked, "What makes you think that?" But we are at a milonga, surrounded by sensuous tango music and how can I think clearly? So, instead I glibly announce that I am older than he.

But that's not the point, of course not! It has nothing to do with logic, this suffering at the passage of time. I think, "Gather ye rosebuds while ye may," but that seems hopelessly dated. Besides at our age we don't think of rosebuds. I know it's a metaphor, but still, it evokes 16-year-old "maidens." I think that the poem is called "To the Virgins, To Make Most of Time." Well, that's not us. The other line that comes to me is from "To His Coy Mistress": The grave's a fine and private place/But none I think/ Do there embrace". That sounds like a proposal. I do whisper it, but it's swallowed up by the music. Anyway, he only hears what he chooses to hear. My own words are inadequate.

On the drive downtown, I too feel melancholy. I think of my 20-year-old granddaughter and am overcome with the memory of her, the few weeks after her birth, of kissing her fragrant little head, before bringing her to her mother, who gently stroked her and whispered endearments while nursing her. But it was just yesterday, that I would sit by her crib, just watching her sleep.

It's my first time back to tango after my surgery and it isn't going well. My feet are screaming, and it all seems like a lot of work. We are not flowing together tonight. Do I have another five years to dance? How long do I live after that, maybe in a wheelchair, moving my torso and my arms to the music, tapping my feet, if I can? I am reading all the time these weeks after the 2016 election. It has always been my escape, that and writing in my diary, in my father's discarded daily planners, when I was a child, later on, in any notebook that came to hand.

The political climate these days frightens me. I see White Supremacists giving the Hitler salute on the TV news. I get glimpses of my parents, of how young and vulnerable they were when fleeing from Nazi Germany. They weren't much older than my granddaughter. The brutal sound of the Gestapo's storm troopers' boots resounds in my ears. I am overcome with sorrow for them. Their trauma lodges in my gut, undigested fear and anger. Will I die in peace, surrounded by well-wishers? We are still relatively safe here in the US, in New York. When I think of illness or surgery, of what comes with age, I remind myself that at least doctors and friends normally mean to help, not to torture us. In that sense we are still safe.

55. CACTUS SOUP

The alarm clock sounds shrill this morning. I let it ring for a while before slowly disengaging myself from my warm comforter. It's 8:15 a.m. and it has been a busy night in dreamland. There have been no traces of romantic Hollywood scenarios. That's not it at all. At five a.m., when I briefly surfaced and turned up the heat, I was aware of a slew of anxiety dreams. They weren't about driving, as one might have expected, considering an adventure the day before. They seemed to cluster around the usual scenario of trying to vainly find and contact the important people in my life. But now the extra few minutes in bed shake loose another dream memory: of being served delicious soup, made out of cactus leaves. In the same vein there is an old woman perched up in a flowering tree, picking tomorrow's lunch maybe. She's up too high and it seems perilous. Sure, enough there is an ominous thud. The many detective movies I watch in which someone gets pushed off a high building are infiltrating my dreams. But wait, there is a happy ending here. No medical examiner needs to be summoned. There is a soft bed under the tree and a young man has landed unharmed. Is the old woman still up in the tree, or has she been transmuted into a young man? A fantasy of mine is of being reborn as a young man, strong and handsome and a Resistance fighter.

On the assumption that every character in a dream represents a part of me, I must be the old woman in the tree as well as the young man. So, part of me lands safely, but I am afraid a lot, vaguely anxious too much of the time. Speaking of things out of my comfort zone, just getting into my car makes me anticipate a collision. But then there is the soup made from so little, from an arid plant and so delicious. And there is the safe landing. Alexey reminds me: "It's the struggle that counts," and perhaps it does yield fruit, if only cactus soup. Dancing last night after driving along the unfamiliar East Side, after the long search for parking, was better than any kind of metaphoric soup or even better than a flowering tree, at least for me.

56. HALLOWEEN SOCIAL

It's raining cats and dogs. In French, they say, "It's dogs' weather"–*Il fait un temps de chien*. I don't know how animals come into this and the thought of cats and dogs falling from the sky is too spooky to consider. There is also "a wind advisory in effect," with warnings of possible gusts of 50 mph. No, I can't really drive downtown to the dance in this weather. But by five p.m., I have changed my mind. You should never listen to weather reports. They're always overblown (yes, pun intended). If the Sawmill River Parkway is closed, I will turn back. It's open, but visibility is nil. I keep visualizing newsreels of recent hurricanes and images of cars floating in the water. I am gripping the steering wheel. I get beeped a lot, but I make my slow way downtown.

I get there at the same time as Miguel. We are both relatively early. The organizer of the social, hugs and greets all comers. She says, "What rain? What are they talking about?" There is a couple sitting at the table in front of us, wearing Superman, Superwoman outfits. I wonder why they are dressed in this odd way. Then I remember it's Halloween. The dances usually have a theme, but I routinely ignore that aspect of the festivities. I thought it was silly that a man was wearing a beret for "French Night."

As the evening wears on, more people arrive wearing costumes. I wonder to Miguel: "How come most of us don't bother with costumes? It is our chance to impersonate someone other than our usual selves for a few hours". Hmm, what or who would I like to be? Would that be a part of myself I would be reluctant to show to other people? Miguel says, "Whenever we get dressed, we are putting on a costume." Well, of course he is right. There are many acceptable choices, nowadays, especially in NYC. I tend to be self-conscious and I wish I could be more imaginative, bolder. I need a dresser or fashion consultant. Even if that were remotely possible, I would probably argue for something bland, an outfit that allows me to blend into the background. Well, there is also the exhibitionist part of me! Do I dare? No, that skirt is too short or too showy. In ordinary life, I opt for comfort every time, for instance, sensible shoes, long skirts, usually black or navy blue. Years ago, my daughters talked of a style of couture they called "interesting Jewish woman," with long gipsy skirts and lots of chunky, ethnic jewelry. I almost made the cut, but not quite because of my reluctance to wear "interesting" jewelry.

Anyway, at about nine p.m., I see Ella and Tony come in wearing eye-catching costumes. Tony explains that he is meant to be Casanova. He looks sleek and elegant. But Ella is Dona Ana, fabulous in a black gown, slightly shorter in front, trailing in back with fitted lace bodice and a shiny silver eye mask. She's incandescent with joy, dances with abandon. We do a shimmy to samba music together, though I am not in costume, only in my usual sober way, wearing a short black skirt with horsehair flounces. Months ago, in a two-minute-long conversation on the dance floor, tonight's stunning Dona Ana told me that she is or was Orthodox Jewish. This dress is setting her free. There is nothing orthodox or even conservative about her tonight. Wow! "Clothes maketh the woman." Maybe I should try a costume next year!

57. BOOTS ARE MADE FOR DANCING

It's the kind of night where there is a scratch on the cha cha CD, and it keeps jumping and I keep wondering why I am off the beat. But it all goes sideways earlier, before I even leave the house. I look dowdy in my mid-calf-length skirt and generic black top. I am having a bad hair week and my lower back is sending out sharp pain signals. I think about cancelling, but it hurts more when I sit, and I can't walk around the house all night. So, I get ready, best I can. I can't wear eye makeup because I have an unattractive eye infection. I don't like bright red lipstick, but I need some color. Sometimes I like my face, never mind the wrinkles or the bags under my eyes. Tonight, I avoid the mirror.

The drive downtown is uneventful, until I notice that I am out of gas. Luckily there is a Mobil Station on Ninth Avenue and 31st Street. I pull out my wallet from my shoe bag and, to my dismay, "no shoes!" I remember feeling that I was travelling somewhat light tonight and doing a mental check: money, food (Miguel's sandwich), shoes. Yes, I have the bag, but no shoes. I remember taking my practice shoes out of the bag (if only I had left them there). Evidently, I forgot to replace them with my social dance shoes, a small-heeled shoe that can be seen as either a little girl's or an old woman's. So here I am wearing UGGS and panicking. I call Miguel on his home phone and then on his cell to see whether we should scrap dancing in these clods and just meet for a drink. He doesn't answer, so when I get caught in traffic on 31st Street going East, I try again. I end up dancing in my boots, feeling clumsy. The ratio of fun to ordeal shifts depending on the dance. The tango, where you need to glide and dance on the ball of the foot, feels just about impossible and by 9:30, I am ready to call it quits.

Of course, on the way home, I get off at the wrong exit (how could I?) and am lost. I plug in my GPS, but can't see the screen, with lights on or off, with or without glasses. I push the screen at random and do end up on the Sprain Parkway and at the Hartsdale exit. After that there are all kinds of mysterious directions to unknown destinations. I am not up to further adventures tonight and they are bound to be undesirable, given how the night is going. Fortunately, eventually there are enough familiar landmarks, even for me in this demented state. I get home and gratefully take off my clumsy boots. At least I have avoided the strain of putting on and taking off shoes. In fact, my back feels a little less sore. I will examine my face in the mirror tomorrow for whatever changes occur, daily and hourly, in my view of myself.

58. FATHER'S DAY

So many memories of my father crowd in, one view pushes aside the previous one. Mornings at exactly eight a.m., he would sit down at the kitchen table, clapping his hands three times, saying "One, two three: where is the coffee?" This was said in German, thus making it more authoritative. He was also fluent in French and English, but German was, after all, his mother tongue. I liked his mischief. I remember him in his late 80s, trying to ride a child's bike and falling down. He widened his eyes in surprise. Raising his eyebrows, he said, "Don't tell your mother!" In my favorite photo of him, taken at a Summer resort in the Catskills, he is wearing a T-shirt and a straw hat. With his head thrown back, he appears to be sitting on a laughing young woman's lap. She is pouring the contents of some bottle into his mouth. It must have been quite a party!

I have never seen him drunk. He tended to be aloof, stern. He held himself erect, impeccably dressed, the perfect stereotype of a German Jewish Doctor. My friends were intimidated by him, a bit afraid, as was I. His contempt and angry judgment made me shrivel. My mother blamed his German mother for his coldness. I never saw him cry. What drove him? He would answer a patient's call at any time, night or day, with patience and concern, no matter how trivial the complaint. At his Memorial, his secretary told a story. She recalled that one day, she confronted him about his system of putting a red paperclip on a patient's chart if he hadn't paid his bill. There were a large proportion of paper clips. She said to him, "Is this any way to run a business?" He drew himself up to his full height and replied, "This is not a business!" I like that story and wonder whether my own inability to charge my psychotherapy patients an adequate fee was in some way influenced by his lofty attitude. I know that in his first job (or should I name it a holy calling?) as an associate in a practice in Harlem, he often gave impoverished patients treatment and medication for free.

He was a good physician, a difficult husband and father. Yet, he was protective and generous with me, anxious about my wellbeing in his way. During our visits, he would draw me into a light filled book lined room. The room used to have a white piano, which he played for many years. He used to talk about playing in movie theaters for the silent films in his youth. In a corner of the room sat his complicated Hi-Fi equipment, which no one but he was allowed to touch. Of course, there was a large collection of classical music CDs: Chopin, Beethoven Schubert, Mozart, opera, the traditional repertoire. There also was a large desk, at which my father used to write checks and at which my mother presided, after his death. When he called me into the room, he would ask, "Do you need money?" I would always say that I was fine, but he would write me a handsome check anyway. He would also at those times bemoan the fact that he didn't insist I become a doctor, like himself. Both my husbands resented these colloquies. Martin used to say he couldn't compete with my father. Paul complained that my father was in love with me. When my father's hand became unsteady, he would ask me to write in the amount.

I liked that room and often escaped from family tensions and gloominess by going in to look at the books and, after my father's death, choosing CDs to take home. Late into his illness I brought him a portable CD player with earphones. I can still see him sitting in his brown velour recliner, gaunt, but his face alive. He listened for a few minutes, said, "It's beautiful," removed the earphones, and after that there no longer was music in the house.

When he descended into dementia in his nineties, a softer side of him emerged. He no longer recognized my mother and was kinder to her. On my visits, he would look at me curiously, until, when I would be ready to leave, he suddenly knew me and told me he loved me. He would then ask me to stay. I remember his cold hands and my urgent desire to leave. After he died, my mother said, "I was afraid you hated him." No, I didn't hate him. I feared him; I was disappointed in his inability to really see me. I admired him. I felt his sadness, his anxiety, his longing for connection behind his frosty demeanor, his angry rants.

59. ALL KINDS OF DANCERS

Sometimes Alexey and Natalya rent out their large brightly lit dance studio. The floor buckles a little at one end but there's plenty of room for socials or group lessons. We all tend to depend on the mirror that lines one side of the room. When we perform in another venue, there usually isn't a mirror, no way of checking out your partner's lead. Oops, where am I? In what direction am I supposed to turn?

When I go for a lesson, I check for Alexey's car in the parking lot. When there's no grey SUV with a lot of fives in the license plate and no light in the studio, I assume, sometimes wrongly, that no one is there, that I have gotten there too early.

Sometimes, even if I think no one is there, I ring the bell and am buzzed in, by a young slender brunette, Linda, who is teaching a heavy-set man in chinos and a grey sweatshirt. She's friendly and we've gotten acquainted. She greets me and comments on my routines. One time, Alexey is late, and she offers to stay with me, in case I'm worried about being alone. People tend to be protective of me as I am getting on in years and look fragile. Some also offer me a seat on the train. I wish I didn't look quite so much like a senior, but I appreciate the kindness. Periodically I remind myself, as a consolation of sorts, "Everyone gets old."

Other times, I see short, curly-headed Art at the studio, teaching a woman who looks bewildered. I know him from socials, and we have danced together several times. He doesn't say hello. Alexey says that he has no idea what Art is doing, but in any case, "it is totally wrong." Often Natalya is teaching. Sometimes it's a couple about to be married. They practice a routine that will wow all the wedding guests. What a good test of their commitment. Can they stay in step with each other? Can they be patient? Most couples seem to enjoy the process, with the occasional moments of frustration, where one or the other has to repeat the step multiple times.

If I get there before eight p.m. on a Wednesday evening, an attractive Black woman in leotards, tights and sneakers will be conducting an aerobics class. Loud rhythmic rock music is blasting from a boom box and about 20 women are moving with varying levels of energy, grace and musicality. It looks like fun. I would like to join the class, but I need sneakers and I also need to be 20 years younger. On Monday morning, Beth, a svelte modern dancer, conducts a Pilates class. I used to take a dance exercise class with her, but it was too early in the morning for me to get there and be alert since I tend to wake up at night. Today, just as my samba technique lesson with Natalya comes to an end, little Asian girls in leotards come streaming in. They must be five to seven years old. They seem very excited, while waiting for the lesson to start. Some chatter away. Two little girls are practicing full splits, as I look on with envy and delight. Most have pink tights and leotards. One of the group has a dance skirt. One has a silver butterfly-shaped barrette in her hair. They all have long red sashes wound around their waists and trailing on the floor. The room fills up as more girls arrive. Their parents in down jackets and boots sit on the benches or stand in the doorway. There's obviously a lot of car-pooling or everyone couldn't fit. I look for my coat, my boots, and my dance bag. I should leave, but I am intrigued. I ask one of the mothers what kind of dance the children are doing. She says they are practicing for the Chinese New Year, which is on February seventh, which is also the day of our bi-annual showcase. I linger in the doorway, watch the teacher lead the class in a graceful ballet warm-up. A boy, maybe 12 years old, a brother of one of these delicate fairies, hoots in derision and is quickly silenced by one of the parents. The children make their red sashes slither snake-wise across the floor. The little dancers flutter from one end of the room to the other.

It snowed all day yesterday. We had a foot of snow, but we are all here… the teachers, me, and all the little ballerinas and their parents. I was planning to go downtown to dance at a milonga tonight. Alexey warns that the temperature will drop, and everything will freeze over. I reluctantly decide to heed his advice and go home, thinking of the little Chinese dancers flying across the Kirsanov's dance studio, like birds.

60. BRA SHOPPING

My daughter Genevieve and I end up in an Irish pub. She orders a tall frothy beer and greasy fish and chips. I have an indifferent hamburger and so-so sweet potato fries. I read the sign on the wall over her head. It says, "Be good to your children. They will choose your nursing home." She gives the tall, Irish waiter the eye. When I pay the bill, he looks at her and thanks her. I say to her, "He's your type, isn't he? Nordic-looking, like your father? She smiles, "Yeah, he's not your type. I know you like the dark Latin ones." He may be 30-years old, if that much. I am prompted to say, "No, but I wouldn't throw him out of bed." "You would be stupid to do that," she says.

We've spent the previous hour wandering around Macy's lingerie section, looking for a bra that will work with the plunging, backless outfit that I am renting from Natalya for this coming Sunday's showcase. When I explain the specification to a sales assistant (I think that's what they are called these days), she makes a face and sends us to racks of padded monstrosities. So, by the time we get to the Irish pub, we are giddy with fatigue. It's dusty and hot in July in New York City. Genevieve has gotten up at five a.m. to take the bus from Maine to get here. My feet don't hurt as much as I expected, but I needed the Irish waiter, the cool, dimly lit Pub, and a glass of iced water. We then walk the long block to Victoria's Secret. There is construction and no sidewalk. Genevieve leads me in a single file, in front of her. In the store, we spot a shimmering, black lace confection. The price tag says $400. Can that be? Yes, so it is. We move on. Finally, with help from a more sophisticated sales associate, I find something that might do. Genevieve ducks out, getting away from the throng of shoppers and the scent of sweet perfume, while I rummage through my backpack for glasses, credit card, driver's license.

We have tickets to The Joyce Theatre, for a dance performance. Once outside, we try to hail a cab, but settle for the subway. Genevieve's subway map reading skills turn out to be, well, not so great. Mine are non-existent, so I let her lead the way. We end up on West Fourth Street and scramble up and down stairs to get a train going in the opposite direction. We arrive at the theatre, both of us, feeling rumpled and sweaty,

I, clutching my Victoria's Secret bag, hoping to not leave it behind. We settle into out orchestra seats. This is to be a rare treat for both of us! The music squeals and groans around us. We look at each other. Genevieve fashions tissue paper ear plugs and hands me some. I breathe a sigh of relief when the first piece is over. The program tells us that the theme is alchemy, and we are to see incarnations of Fire, Earth, Air and Water. Dancers in red tights and leotards are tilting phallic posts around the stage. I think about getting my money back, but then we settle into the spectacle. It is marvelous, after all.

After, I remember to take my hard-won new bra, but I never wear it, opting for a different costume. It is less glamorous, but I like it. Genevieve comes to see me dance. She doesn't need ear plugs. She helps with my costume changes. She applauds and tells me that I'm "great." I love a discriminating audience!

61. THE BOOK OF DANIEL

Years ago, I put the book down after reading only a few chapters. This time, I am determined to read Doctorow's *The Book of Daniel*. What made me stop reading it last time? I remember being disturbed by Daniel's sadism towards his wife. Daniel is the imaginative re-creation of the Rosenberg's son. It was, I suppose, sadism "light," compared to the government's imprisonment of his parents and their execution in the electric chair when he was roughly 11-years old and his sister six-years old. It is a fictionalized version of events, but it doesn't detract from its power. Doctorow goes back and forth in time from one paragraph to the next. It feels right because we live the accumulation of our lives at any one moment, I think. The book is brilliant, disturbing in its evocation of dull, impoverished interiors, of sitting shiva for the half-crazed but suffering grandmother, the outing to hear Paul Robeson and the sudden, almost lethal violence. No one survives the final cataclysm unscathed; of course, they don't. The book begins with Daniel's visit to his practically catatonic sister in a psychiatric hospital. This time, I have trouble putting the book down. It's an old paperback with the pages turning brown at the edges and the print is too small. Still, I have to forcibly tear myself away to get ready for tonight's dance social. I want to finish the novel because it fascinates me and also because I want to move away from the experience that Doctorow has so powerfully re-created.

Still, it is time to shower, get dressed and move into a different reality. I choose a dress that I haven't worn in a long time, navy blue with a fitted bodice and a short flare skirt. I drive downtown and enter a room illuminated with strobe lights and gaiety. I am a different person now, attuned to the music, to my partner, to the movement of my hips. I tell Miguel something about the novel, as we dance. I tell him about my idea of time, of a lifetime compressed into a single moment. He argues that a moment can exist detached from everything else. We agree that it is difficult to be truly in the present. We are moving to the insistent beat of a hustle, an odd moment for this kind of discussion. The music and the dance engulf me. For now, I am joyous, free of the past, free of history; tragedy tangential, an afterthought.

62. OUT OF STEP

Miguel and I are out of sync on the dance floor tonight. Something isn't working. We are not connecting. I feel that I keep chasing him, in an effort to follow, and that I can't catch up. He says that I move out of the frame, away from him and that I keep turning my head. I stumble, thrown off balance. Am I off balance? I saw a video that used tango as a metaphor for relationship. He leads, she follows, but maintains her individuality, and then sometimes she leads. Both people are attuned to each other's movements, to each other's feelings. We're not even communicating tonight. I try to keep my eyes fixed on his face. Emil has told us to look at our partner's nose to keep oriented. It seems silly, but it works, up to a point. So, I really "see" Miguel's face now. He looks unhappy, almost desolate, alone in his world. He doesn't smile much in general. Anyway, you're not supposed to smile when you dance tango. It's about heartbreak, loss, blood on the floor. But this isn't just a "tango look." I ask him about how he feels. He assumes I am enquiring about his wonky knee and says he is fine. On the way out, in the elevator, I rephrase my question and tell him that I thought he looked gloomy. He seems surprised and says that maybe it is just that his energy is low.

On the other hand, the atmosphere is particularly festive at TangoMania today. People greet me enthusiastically. I barely know the names of some of the dancers who hug me and kiss me on the cheek. Maybe, though it's all very superficial, I am part of this tango community. I don't know why but I don't fit easily into any group, so it is gratifying to be recognized and to be welcomed. There is live music today, always a thrill for dancers. A musician plays the bandoneon and there's a keyboardist and a singer who sings a lush rendition of "Melena." A couple, who tied for World Champions at a competition in San Francisco, performs to thunderous applause.

Miguel and I sometimes flow together effortlessly, but often lately, there is a struggle. I am distracted, my mind wanders. I admire some other couple's style or a woman's flowing dress or her bright green spike heeled tango shoes, that I will never be able to wear. I also wonder which ones of the couples are sleeping together. You should be able to tell, but maybe it's just the better dancers who look, as though they are passionate in bed. When I don't pick up Miguel's signals in a particular figure, he explains. I somewhat resent being taught at a milonga. Still, his words help, and I can do it the second time around. Partners should talk to one another, but it ruins the mystique of the wordless embrace of tango. Also, I should be focusing on my partner, not on stiletto heels.

The nights we do ballroom feel more spontaneous, more joyous, though of course it took ten years of lessons to get me to that point. There is more room for self-expression, especially in the Latin. His lead is subtle and clear. The dance is sexy, sensual. We show off for each other. I love to watch him, his grace, his creativity. He plays with the rhythms. Following him, feeling the music is entirely natural. I am vaguely aware of the other dancers, but nothing really matters, except for the music and Miguel and our nonverbal conversation.

But tonight, I feel disconnected from Miguel with whom I have been dancing almost five years. He could be miles away. Are we even friends? I am not completely myself with him. I curb my demonstrative persona in his presence. I mirror his demeanor. Just now, I can't even get in touch with my secret affection for him. When we talk on the phone later that week, he has figured out what ails him. So much gets buried in the silences between us. We do an uneasy *pas de deux* all these years. We talk with each other at times. I feel closer to him and then he pulls back into the shadows. Instead of pursuing him, I follow his lead, until he comes towards me again.

His disappearances leave me disappointed. Is he mindful of this dance? It doesn't work well for tango. The ideal, achieved by some partners, some of the time, is to move as one person, being totally in touch with the other person's mood. How often does this happen in life or on the dance floor, even for soul mates or lovers? Is it even likely with two people who are "just friends?"

63. LOVE AND DANCE

My young friend, Nari, moved to Ottawa, to work for the Korean Embassy about a year ago. She filmed my showcases for several years and we collaborated on the English version of her book about Alaska. I enjoyed getting together with her, whenever her busy young professional's schedule allowed.

She hasn't been in touch, except for the occasional sightings on Facebook. Oh well, I say to myself, we do live such different lives, in different generations, different cultures. She's Born-Again Christian. I am a superannuated Jewish Atheist. But this week, I get a message from her. She would be in New York City for Easter. She writes, "Do you still go to Manhattan to dance on Sundays? Could we get together? Can I bring my boyfriend?" I remember her laughingly telling me that he is more religious than she is.

I decide that I had better dress modestly for our coffee meeting, though I am going dancing afterwards. I am careful not to wear an overly short skirt with slits and to avoid a top that verges on the décolleté. We meet in front of the studio. I see her waving from down the block. I don't know what to expect of the boyfriend, don't even know his name. He turns out to be a slender, graceful Korean man, guileless, open, very young. The two of them obviously have a secret, that they're dying to tell me. They smile, laugh, give each other looks, one prompting the other to speak. In the middle of a conversation and reminiscences, I find myself asking parental questions: "What do you do? What are you studying?" We all giggle a little. We know what this is about. They are getting married and this is a rehearsal for the more important interview with the Korean parents. I am charmed, tell them stories about my young husband asking for my hand in marriage, 57 years ago.

I leave almost reluctantly to meet Miguel at the dance. Still elated, I tell him all about it. He wishes he had been part of the parental interview. I see an elderly couple on the dance floor. They were here last week as well. He is bent over. They move gingerly, shuffling their feet. They lean into each other, their heads touching. We are whirling around them but are caught up in their aura. They are happy, they are in love.

64. CULTURAL DIFFERENCES?

Dora is Japanese. She says that in her culture you're supposed to blend in, you're not supposed to stand out or show off. She and I do dance showcases with Alexey twice a year; but right now, we are at our every-other-week meeting during which four Japanese women take turns reading in English from a novel. I help with pronunciation and obscure meanings. Their English is good, but there are occasional questions.

Right now, we are reading Irvin Yalom's *Love's Executioner*, a series of psychotherapy tales. To my surprise, they love it. I try to pick something interesting, but not too challenging to read. So far, we have read *Never Let Me Go*, *Gone Girl*, and *Angel, Angel*. All of this leads to interesting discussions about our personal experiences and about cultural differences. When I leave to take a break, the group lapses seamlessly into their mother tongue. My Japanese is non-existent.

So, today, Dora says she doesn't want to stand out. I say, "But you liked it when Miguel said you are a beautiful dancer." I think to myself, "He never said that to me." It doesn't take much for my competitive juices to kick in. Dora says, "When my daughter says, 'You were good Mom,' I want to say: 'More, tell me more.'" She gestures with her hand to emphasize the point. I say that I too am conflicted about being visible, because of my war experience, of having to hide from the Nazis. Maybe we are not so different after all. Still there is something to all this. Mei shares that when she used to go to PTA meetings, the teacher would be mystified that she wanted her child to just be ordinary. She adds that American parents want their children to be special, to be very successful. Also, the Japanese woman is taught to denigrate her own accomplishments. I am reminded of a scene in one of Ang Lee's films, where the non-Chinese boyfriend is invited to dinner. The hostess says, "I think this dish is too salty." The guest makes the faux pas of saying, "Yes, maybe it is a bit salty." We all laugh. I am reminded that my family is often annoyed with me, when I announce that something, I have cooked may not be so good. Apparently, I do this "all the time." Maybe I am part Asian!

I know that I announce that I am not such a good dancer, as well. Of course, it is true that I am not up to Dora's level. She works hard at her technique but says she doesn't compare herself with others. She routinely does at least ten dances at the show and wears sparkling dance costumes. I make do with more ordinary dresses and am challenged enough with doing three show dances and two or more warm-up dances. One time our dances appeared on the same DVD. It was painful for me to watch because she was so much better than I. I found myself fast forwarding her dances and feeling disgusted with my efforts.

Alexey says, "Just do your personal best." He is right of course, but last time I was frustrated because it wasn't even "my personal best." I admire other people's performances or their inborn talent, but I am jealous, wish my efforts could be more fruitful. Would I feel less competitive, if I were Japanese? I am not sure.

65. JUST PLAY A MERENGUE

Billie Holiday sings "Strange Fruit." No one sings it like she does. "Blood on the leaves/Bodies hanging from the poplar trees/The scent of magnolia." I remember phrases of the lyrics. Mostly I remember the shudder on hearing it, the stone in my heart.

Why can't I write about, say, "Singing in the Rain?" Miguel and I danced a foxtrot to it yesterday and I was thinking of Gene Kelly and also that I might not be able to dance like this in only a few more years. What if Miguel moves to California to be with his family? Would I force myself to go out on my own?

Alexey says: "You're miserable, just play a merengue and move your hips." Sometimes Michael Jackson's version of "Jailhouse Rock," danced freestyle, is the remedy for me. Oops, I mentioned "jail." It's back to the merengue! The day before yesterday, my friend Samuel and I went to a sunny park. A minibus takes you from the parking place to your destination. When the door clanged shut, I thought of jail. Sometimes, on trains, I think of cattle cars on the way to Auschwitz.

So, let's get back to "now," to the dance, shall we, before more of my darker obsessions come spilling out. Here's to foolish complaints. Last night there were too many periods of non-dancing. First, when we arrived, it took time to find a table. Then, in the middle of things, just as I had relaxed and warmed up, Miguel sat down to eat. Then some woman collared him to talk about his teaching at the Y. Apparently, she was a wannabe dance teacher. A woman next to me refused a dance, because she was eating. How can you choose to eat when there's music?

66. THE JOURNEY

The Greek poet Cavafy writes that it is the journey that counts, but I say, "not this Saturday night." There are snow flurries and I have to clean off my new car before setting out. Tonight is its snow baptism. This makes me especially nervous. It's slushy on the highway and visibility is poor. I keep cleaning my windshield, hoping for a better view. There is good jazz on the radio and that helps. I drive slowly but nevertheless I am already on 34th Street in 40 minutes.

I drive across town without incident and start looking for parking spaces on Seventh Avenue. There's a tiny space right across from

Dance Manhattan, where we are to dance, but I know that my car can't fit. Finally, there's something on Madison and it's only a block and a half from my destination. The wind is icy. I cover my ears with my mittened hands. I can't mess up my hair with a hat before the dance. It's okay on the way home. Natalya altered my body-fitting black velvet dress for me, putting in long slits up each of its thighs. I think she got a bit carried away. Sitting in any kind of a demure fashion is out of the question. But, after all, I plan on dancing all night, well two hours with Miguel. He is grooving tonight, so cool, so graceful. I move with him in some kind of enchantment. We are in the zone. It feels as though we are moving as one.

I tell him about being grateful for these hours. He says, "Life doesn't always move in a straight line. You have to enjoy what you can". I do! I do! It's a spirited group tonight. Others are also dancing with abandon. Some people are clowning, laughing, making contact. Yes, it is worth the journey, but it's about being here with the music, with my black dress, with Miguel, with the heat in my belly and with the joy in my heart.

67. ANOTHER BLACK DRESS

Things are fairly predictable in their madness in the Stage Tango class. First, Emil assembles three couples, more or less, who are willing to endure the process of preparing for a show. Some of us get convinced by him that this is a good idea. But here we are in the sixth week of learning an ever-changing choreography, which none of us can remember from week to week. The day before yesterday, Emil says to me, "You are performing next Saturday night." I have a hazy concept of what it is we are supposed to be doing, but I want to get it over with. Driving to New York City on a Sunday is feasible, but getting parking is not. Today, I park in a parking lot. It is expensive, but to avoid being very late again, I give in and give up on the endless search for street parking. Miguel and I are both on time, as are Maria and John, another superannuated couple. Jeb and Carol are late. Carol comes all the way from Orange County. I can't imagine what Emil told her to get her to do this, though he is pretty convincing, or shall I say, "persistent." I don't know what Emil has said to the others, but several times, he told Miguel and me, "You are experienced. You have to look good. The others, they don't know nothing." Great! Miguel is a professional dancer, but even he has trouble pulling together Emil's different ideas. The three couples are supposed to dance in unison. Emil bellows, "No, one couple can't be doing the sentada and the other one is doing castigados. It doesn't work that way." In the middle of this lesson, he is chewing out Maria and John: "You're late! How are they supposed to come in with the music, when you are still doing the kicks?" Maria asks a reasonable question, but he continues on his rant: "You can't just do any step you want. You have to be with the music."

I whisper to Miguel, "Fine, so stop yelling and fix it." Jeb and Carol are new to this. He is a beginner, a young fair man, who later is accused of doing this just to get to sleep with Carol. She is a six-foot tall slender woman, who towers over everyone in the room. She is obviously a dancer but doesn't know much about tango. They are a handy target for Emil's frustration. He is bitterly castigating Jeb, "You don't even know the steps! You are pushing her. Don't push her. She'll fall down. Have you even practiced? Stay for the milonga and practice." It often seems that tango is a dangerous activity, with Emil often warning, "You'll fall. He will kick you. Do you want to be kicked?" At the end of the session, he tells us that we have two more weeks. Evidently, the light dawns: None of us know the choreography! So, we have two more Sundays of schlepping down to the city to "rehearse." It turns out we have even more time, as Maria fractures her toe, trying the steps with John in her living room. But I am getting ahead of the story.

This is the day I try on my sparkly black dress, with the long slit up the leg, to make sure I can dance without losing my strapless bra. I expect accolades. The women are impressed, but Miguel and Emil both complain that I am too thin. Emil says, in his inimitable way: "You look like a scrawny chicken" and says that I should go home and eat three lbs. of pork. Miguel looks at me from the side and says, "Is this the way the dress used to fit you. You used to fill it better. A woman should have hips and some stomach." So, the afternoon is a total success.

Now, two weeks later, the wardrobe situation has shifted. Emil wants us to wear something that moves when we do turns and *sacadas*. So, goodbye, sexy straight dress that supposedly makes me look like "a scrawny chicken." I discuss the options with Miguel. He favors my flapper dress with all the fringes that keep getting stuck on the buttons of his jacket. Also, they keep falling off, as we dance. Whenever I wear it, I bring a backup dress, in case I end up denuded of fringes. No, no, we don't need wardrobe malfunctions. Bad enough that his watch gets stuck on my Capezio mesh stockings on that last dress rehearsal. I have a plain black dance skirt, a little boring, that I can wear. Maria has a fifties' strapless dress, which she is having altered to have straps. We don't need extra problems. We're all supposed to wear the same kind of thing, all black. We are in some kind of Greek or Spanish drama, perhaps, maybe Lorca's *The House of Bernarda Alba*, with its dark, menacing atmosphere. I can't talk about this with Carol. She quit. She's the tall one, from Orange County, remember? Emil tells us that it's because of Jeb, who ends up as *persona non grata*. Emil goes into salacious detail, but I am not sure. It's a good bet that she wanted out of this frenzied madness because of the teacher. In the event, we do the show, with another woman dancing with Emil, who still doesn't know the choreography, as he readily admits. I end up wearing the showy black dress, as Carol's replacement, Natasha, doesn't wear swirly things. I see the video. My black dress is the best part of the show!

68. SURPRISE ME!

Alexey often says to me, "Surprise me!" Last week, I say to him, "Do I ever really surprise you?" As an experienced and intuitive teacher (he is uncanny, actually), he knows so well what we all can do. Yes, some days, I am more distracted, but he knows, instantaneously, when I walk in the door, to what extent I will be able to focus, what percentage of me will really be there. Just as I feel my attention waning, he says, "Focus, stay with me. Don't drift into Naomi-land." Obviously staying focused is a major hurdle. I can't seem to come up with a solution. I order a book, *Meditation for Dummies*, but it never arrives in the mail, as though it's unlikely that I will meditate, be more centered, more present, no matter what I try.

To my question as to whether I ever surprise him, Alexey says: "You surprised me with the purple wig." Well, why not a purple wig? Maybe, now that I am 80 years old, it is time to be more adventurous.

In my group of Japanese readers, *a propos* of a book we are reading, Mei, one of the older women, comments: "In Japan, the old women are wearing vivid colors, outfits in hot pink and large gaudy hats". We all look at each other and see we are wearing either brown, navy blue, or black. She and I, as the oldest, are entitled to wear, purple, red, magenta, chartreuse, bright royal blues, anything that appeals to us. I know that I will never have the nerve, not if I am 90 years old and in Japan, to do that—except for in the showcase.

The purple wig is obviously for the next show, for a hustle number. It goes with my purple bodysuit with bell bottoms, matched with a sparkly silver sequin jacket and belt. Sometimes an adventurous costume can spark my enthusiasm and make up for a less than perfect performance. Julie is bringing her new boyfriend. I have never met him. What do they say about first impressions?

In truth, I haven't been feeling that well for weeks, queasy, tired, a bit depressed. My feet hurt and I start feeling sick a half hour into the lesson. Usually, I can't tempt anyone into coming to the show, even for free. This time six people are coming to see me, and I fear some kind of meltdown, that I will get lost in space and won't remember any of my seven dances. But there is always the purple wig and the silver sequins. Remember the poem: "When I am old, I will wear purple"? (Hot pink, perhaps?) "It's o.k. to wear dull colors, when you are young," says Mei,

"But when you are old, you need color. Those old women, in their finery, look marvelous."

69. LESSONS

Alexey's voice barks out, "Stay! Wait! Heels! Stop! Focus! Stay with me!"

I say, "It sounds as though you are training a dog. Well, maybe it wouldn't be so bad to be a dog. My mother might have liked me better. She loved dogs."

Alexey laughingly quips, "That's a sad story." I am inclined to find it funny, maybe because, just maybe it isn't entirely true. But it would be comforting to be given treats and just about now, it would be nice to have somebody stroke me. He adds, "Smile. You look like you're in a Tolstoy novel, having your leg amputated without anesthesia."

So, now it's time to spot better, make my turns sharper, get my arm further back and higher. There are two more days before show time. A more soothing way to put it would be that, "it's time for the midterm exam" or "it's just part of the process." When Miguel joins me at the show to see the "exam results," he says, "It's the journey that counts." The journey compels me to keep going even through long arid stretches of constant repetition and minimal progress. In the end you do have to present the dances, such as they are, on the designated afternoon. It doesn't help to ask for an extension: "two months, perhaps?" before the last rehearsal, otherwise known as "last hope Saturday." I do every breathing exercise I remember from my years of yoga, waiting for the kundalini to rise, watching for that floating feeling, when giving myself suggestions, such as, "You can do this" might work. I am in control. Breathing is the answer.

Sunday, a few hours before the show, the long-neglected yoga tape is playing, and I am breathing and hoping. Alexey says that you have to go through the dance like a grocery list, ticking off one part after another. Don't get panicked about the whole dance, never mind about the eight dances on the program. He says, as patiently as possible, under the circumstances, "You've driven to the store, you've parked your car. You're not going to turn around and go home because the line is too long." This bit of wisdom might be in response to my warning about "skipping town, getting sick or breaking a leg". I think to myself, "You can't change your mind in the middle of giving birth," but a sudden attack of the flu or a long grocery line sound like legitimate excuses to me. Of course, on Sunday I sort out my four costume changes and my purple wig, remembering hair pins, safety pins and the stunning necklace for one of the dances, as well as the usual rhinestones from the now defunct Loehmann's. Julie will be my dresser. She arrives, beaming, with her boyfriend Joshua and immediately tells me that I look gorgeous. I feel dowdy, even with my makeup. I have been washing my hair, straightening the house and watching *The Americanization of Emily* on Turner Classic Movies and have picked up Miguel at the train at three p.m. We're ready to go. There is no turning back.

70. AVOIDING THE DEATH CAFÉ

Ellen and I first meet and become friends at the dance studio. One day she surprises me by asking, "Do you want to volunteer with me at a Death Café? There's one next Saturday afternoon. It's just a matter of passing around cookies and tea." It's a sunny May day and the prospect of serving refreshments to people who are meeting to talk about death doesn't feel compelling. Remaining in denial about death, just a little longer, seems the more appealing option. Confronting this inevitable stage of life has crossed my mind, of course. I read Irvin Yalom's book *Staring into the Sun*, in which he advocates living fully, as a way of coping with the fear of death. There are also two books on my shelf, both bearing the title The *Denial of Death*, which I do intend to read, soon.

But I associate Ellen with Samba, not death! I see her practicing her Samba walks with Natalya, getting the hang of the bounce of the hips. She does all the dances well, but she does a particularly wicked Samba. She performs with Alexey in glitzy costumes. We really got to know each other at a dance weekend in the Catskills' "Stardust Ballroom." I remember her driving us in her smooth quiet car while we talked. We share a room. We are sisters, companions, and it feels good. The only hitch seems to be that she likes to crank up the air conditioning and I wear layers to avoid shivering in my bed.

You can dance all day here, and into the night. There are lavish Catskill hotel type meals which we share with other obsessed dancers. Everyone is looking out for partners all the time. It adds an edge of excitement and of anxiety. On Saturday, with Ellen's encouragement, I wear my short, empire-style silver lamé dress. She pronounces the dress "fun." We do have fun, though we skip most of the lessons. There are group lessons in everything from Hustle to Argentine Tango. I am somewhat intimidated by group lessons, though I have taken many. Oddly enough, early in my learning, I was asked to demonstrate for Continuing Education dance lessons. That came about through my going to a Greenburgh event which promised lessons by "Antonio." Well, Antonio couldn't make it and I was the only person who showed up. His colleague, a dance teacher named Michelle, led me through some Modern/Jazz moves. It was embarrassing, but after taking a Latin Dance class with Michelle, she thought well enough of me to ask me to demonstrate the man's part for her group, because she had broken a toe. After my initial nervousness, it seemed natural and even pleasurable to lead a simple merengue, salsa or cha cha. Another woman demonstrated the woman's part.

In the usual group lesson configuration, the teacher usually calls for all the "girls" to line up on one side of the room and for all the "guys" to line up on the other side, facing their prospective partners. All women get to be "girls" in perpetuity, or so it seems. It reminds me of the Virginia Reel, which was part of the curriculum in Junior High School, where the gym occupied the same space as the cafeteria. Whenever it comes to mind, I get a strong whiff of Campbell's tomato soup in my nostrils. Everybody gets to try the new step demonstrated by the teacher and you keep switching partners. Sometimes you are on your own. Mercifully, it is because of the gender gap (always more women than men), not because you are being shunned for being too old, too fat, too skinny, too ugly or for having two left feet. Being a new face at an intimate social or being the only single person at a venue attended mostly by couples, of course, also puts you at a disadvantage. I remember once, starting to dance with another enterprising woman, and the organizers telling us to stop, not because she was horrified by the possibility that we might be lesbians, but because she didn't want to give the impression to newcomers that there might not be many men at this party. Not that it takes women that long to figure out the lay of the land.

By Sunday morning, both Ellen and I have had enough. The hotel is in the mountains and the landscape is lush, but nobody ventures out. We are caught up in an obsessive spiral, where the outside world ceases to exist. You can almost hear the clink of the slot machines in Las Vegas. No one thinks of anything but the next dance and the next partner. Nevertheless, we escape somehow, and on the way home, we stop at the next town for coffee, where I buy enormous blue earrings, which I will never wear.

We consider going on another weekend, but it seems to me that my body is not up for the stress of non-stop dancing. Ellen no longer comes to the studio and I miss our talks. Maybe it is time to consider volunteering at the Death Café with her. Someone once told me that you can tolerate everything, if you can hold someone's hand in the dark. Failing that there is music and dance. Ellen still goes dancing every weekend, as I do, throwing herself into the music and the joy of movement, to defeat death, while she also faces its mysteries.

71. PARTINGS

Many students come and go at the dance studio. People move, develop different priorities. There have been instances of new girlfriends resenting their boyfriend's dancing with dazzling Natalya, failing to register that she is an exacting teacher focused on dance technique, not frivolous dalliance. There have also been deaths and illnesses, some incapacitating. When I started taking lessons, thirteen years ago, there was Ann, 85 years old and winning competitions, an inspiration to the younger dancers. To our dismay, one evening, she suffered a stroke and crashed her car on her way to a dance lesson. Her family was puzzled by her dedication to dancing, but until her accident, she never gave up, kept going with the help of an occasional cortisone injection.

Even more startling was the stroke suffered by Joe, a vigorous man in his forties, an athlete, gifted with grace and a sense of rhythm. Several years ago, he arrived a bit late for a showcase in which he was going to perform. He was about to sit down at my table, when he suddenly crashed to the floor. The show proceeded, while paramedics arrived, it seemed, within minutes and then there were the years of struggling to regain mobility. He came to see the show several years later. I was impressed by his bravery, but in the end, it must have been too painful for him to be reminded of what he had to give up. I hope he's better, maybe almost ready to dance again.

For me the most memorable loss was that of Rachel, a vivacious woman who was diagnosed with a recurrence of cancer, now stage-four metastatic breast cancer. She returned for lessons and for show preparation in spite of the illness and the debilitating treatment. I remember sitting with her at a show, before this difficult time, and commiserating with her that friends didn't understand what this meant to us and used every possible excuse to avoid being part of the audience. The day before what was to be her last performance, she had started a new medication which left her feeling nauseous and weak. But that night she was totally in the zone, full of zest and joy in a sparkling Latin costume. We applauded her with love and awe, daring to hope. She died a few months later.

Dance, dance till the end of time!

72. LEONARD COHEN

A few years ago, my grandson Adam and I gave each other an identical present, Leonard Cohen's last CD, *You Want It Darker*. I am listening to it these days, mostly in the evenings. It is his farewell to the world. I am immediately overcome with the solemnity of his tone. He sings: "Hineni. I am ready, My Lord." There are echoes of his traditional Orthodox Jewish upbringing, but also threads of other sacred music, as well as of his leaving behind his worldly preoccupations.

I gave the CD to Adam, who is twenty, and just beginning his life, because it was the newest and, alas as it happens, the last of Leonard Cohen's creations. Adam is no stranger to emotional pain, but hopefully there haven't yet been for him "intimations" of mortality. For me, as I slide, year by year, month by month perhaps closer to the end, there's awe and joy at a man's leaving poetry, song, beauty behind for the world.

Lately, I feel the need for something sacred for inspiration to help me live, not yet to die. I am far from ready. There's never been God for me, just beauty and love. But I want words I can repeat to myself every morning, to remind myself to be grateful, to take in life, to be joyous when I can. It does sound like what I am after is a prayer, doesn't it? Words can inspire, whether spoken to a deity or to yourself. So, what is my mantra, my prayer, my thing of beauty? Perhaps: "Be kind! Love well! It is not necessary to create. It is enough to listen, to look, to read, mostly to keep your heart open." Thank you, Leonard Cohen. You live so intensely in your farewell.

73. JOY

I say to Miguel, as we sit down for a few minutes at our designated table, "Being human is complicated." We have snippets of conversation between dances, when we lean in and whisper into each other's ears in order to be heard. When we got up to dance at yesterday's Social, I shared a different sudden insight: "Joy is simple." It is pure joy, to watch him move, completely alive, a true dancer.

Our last dance is a foxtrot. I say to him, "Just like Fred and Ginger, right?" I am joking, but it feels as though we are gliding effortlessly.

Everything else disappears and we are in the zone. Everything else is complicated, even unconditional love.

74. EVERYTHING IS CANCELLED

Everything is cancelled these last three days. My last big outing on Christmas Eve was for a milonga, enticingly called "The Red and Black Ball." It was glamorous, red and black and festive. Now, I am marooned in my quiet house. I even forget to play music. Alexey is the only person that I see this weekend, as I can't miss my lesson/rehearsal for the February Showcase. On Thursday, snow is drifting, trees are whipping around madly, and it is bitter cold. By the afternoon, when I see that I can't open my front door, I realize that I was right to cancel my tango lesson downtown. Miguel, I know, is riding his bike through the storm, but he is tougher than I.

On Friday, my Japanese readers' group cancels. It is only because I went to DiCicco's on Wednesday to buy Bahlsen's chocolate-covered cookies for them that I even knew that a storm was coming. These quiet days, when nobody comes and the outside feels alien and frozen, I read, I struggle through Spanish grammar, watch too much TV, make babaganoush and lentil soup. I talk on the phone and write emails to stay connected and for one hour there is always Alexey. He is Russian and no brutal weather is likely to stop him. I do freeze getting in and out of the car on the way to the studio and I can't imagine getting dressed up to go dancing on Sunday night. My peer group had cancelled in the morning. I decide they have a point and decide not to go dancing. I am sorry the rest of the evening, puttering around the house, fantasizing how lovely it would be to be wrapped in a tango embrace. I could have worn fleece pants under my dress. There are warming booths on the train platform, once the wind blows you in their direction. I wouldn't attempt to drive, but really, I would be safe on the train, wouldn't I?

75. BIRTHDAY GIFT

It's time to party! A surprise two-disc set of Aretha Franklin music arrived at my door today in an Amazon envelope. It's a few days after my birthday and it could be a gift, from a secret admirer, perhaps. It's blasting from my little boom box and I'm dancing, moving my hips, singing along. I am almost certain it wasn't you, Francis, who sent it. You are forbidden to write to me and you've never been a person to remember birthdays, unless prompted and I am not there to prompt you. Still, it's reminding me of all the afternoons we listened to music together in my dining area with you dancing in the kitchen, me joining you and singing, off tune, probably, but you always thought it was marvelous. We did have fun boogie-ing. We

were often looking for music for a performance.
No one loved applause more than you. Do you
remember? For me Aretha rocks even more when
I think of those days.

76. LAST HOPE SATURDAY

Dora tells me, "If it snows, I am not coming."
    "What do you mean, you won't come?
You have got to be kidding me! You have to
come! O.K., so, you're afraid of driving, so am I.
I will pick you up!"
    Dora is one of the best dancers in the
group and is likely to be a third of the show. We
keep running into each other at lessons. We have
this joke/fear that she and I are the only people
dancing. Definitely, I can't be the only one
dancing. The event *has* gotten much smaller,
over the years, with fewer dancers doing multiple
dances and a shrinking audience. It snows on
Friday. We keep our fingers crossed for Sunday.
The roads are clear. "So, Dora, you have no
excuses." Twisted ankles. the flu, sore knees and
panic don't fly as reasons to not turn up. Neither
does weather, as far as I am concerned.
    Last winter, in time for the show, the
roads were a sheet of ice. Julie, who has a sturdy
car, offers to drive, but with obvious trepidation.
She says, making me feel really guilty, "So, you
want to get us all killed? Why can't they cancel
it?" We have to go. I have been preparing for six
months, with four lessons per week. So, Miguel,

Francis, Diana and I cautiously make our way to Julie's car. When it's all over, I will go flying on the ice on the way from the car to my house. I am saved from a major fall by grabbing on to the lamp post, which luckily is steady enough not to come crashing down with me.

Most everyone gets there, to Alexey and Natalya's palpable relief. There was a celebratory feel to the evening. We were united in our heroism. After hugs all around, we did Natalya's salsa warm up. There aren't enough men (or leaders) for general dancing, so the group is the next best thing. I always need a lot of warm up and, besides, I want to have fun, so I have been inviting Miguel to come for several years now. To some extent I dance for him. As a dancer he can judge whether I am making progress. So, more pressure not to mess up. Francis comes for every show as well. Julie tells me that I blatantly ignore him, while making eyes at Miguel. Conscience-stricken, I check in with Francis. Apparently, he doesn't register any discomfort about the situation. I vaguely realize that there's something off about my behavior. Still my main concern is Alexey's admonition. "Make me proud."

Fortunately, this winter, the roads have been cleared of snow for my last rehearsal before the show. Alexey likes to call this "Last hope Saturday." The studio is busy that day, as one nervous student after the other tries to get the routine right, finally. For the last month of rehearsal, Alexey likes to remind everyone how many weeks, days, and then hours are left before show time. He is increasingly gleeful as we get closer to performance time. He loves it when the excitement peaks. Adrenaline can make me focus, but it can just as easily drive me into a frenzy of nerves, where it feels that I don't remember any part of the carefully repeated choreography, not even how it starts. At one of my earlier shows, I stop in the middle, look at Alexey and say, "Wait, did we leave out something?" Disastrous!! Of course, we didn't leave anything out. It's Alexey we are talking about. He never forgets anything, down to the flower you are supposed to attach to your dress. And anyway, you have to keep dancing, no matter what. Fake it, if you have to! He'll rescue you somehow, lead you into something familiar. The audience doesn't know or won't admit knowing that you've screwed up. On that occasion, Samuel copies my DVD for me and expunges my sudden startled stop. Perfect!

I don't aim for "perfect" for the dances, but I am panicked as "last hope Saturday" comes all too soon, in spite of a month's postponement. I never feel prepared enough, but my costumes are all sorted out by the last week. I am wearing a glitzy black and red off-the-shoulder dress, very short on one side. I keep wondering about wardrobe dysfunctions as one leg feels bare. This dress is for my so-called "warm up dances," the cha cha and the rumba routines, which in fact I don't know that well and which cause me a certain amount of anxiety. These are the open gold routines for competitions, but we all do them at our own level. Doing our "personal best." Still, I wish I could come close to doing as well as Dora, or Lila, or Judith.

I am repeating the show dance that I messed up six months ago. People liked it, but I know that I froze at the beginning and at the end, during two of the sections Alexey and I do side by side. I got disoriented by being in a space other than the studio and suddenly didn't know which way to turn. I envisioned that particular scenario in my dreams. You don't necessarily want all your dreams to come true! It's a piece choreographed to an electronic version of the theme music for "Mission Impossible". It has felt "impossible" that I wouldn't repeat my mistakes this time, though we've rehearsed every single lesson so it would feel entirely non-threatening this time around. I am wearing a black mock turtleneck leotard with my flowing, black Eileen Fisher pants and a dramatic rhinestone necklace that must be pinned. Last time, it was flying all over as I danced, especially when he was spinning me upside down. Alexey was displeased about this. To this day I feel that it was the least of my problems. In rehearsal, Alexey keeps stressing, "Turn more, more, more. Your feet not turned out, on that second Paso Doble turn." I am trying, but mostly I hope that my body will remember which way to turn at crunch time. We don't practice the lifts and the drops, until the few weeks before the show, to avoid extra wear and tear on my body. The challenge is to land on time and to move right in rhythm to the next step.

Then, of course, there's the new dance, to a drum piece, with a new-agey, interesting soundtrack. I am cued sometimes by Alexey's whispered instructions, sometimes by phrases, such as, "they dance the moon and the stars," or "realize your rhythm," which leads into the section with the tricky turns, which were almost cut. I am wearing a purple, form-fitting bodysuit with large bell bottoms. I found it in a costume shop in Portland during my yearly visit to Genevieve. We always do a lot of poking around consignment shops, looking for costumes and dance dresses when I visit. This time we were hot on the trail for something that would work for "Realize Your Rhythm" and we find it. We even get it at half price, as the owner likes Genevieve. Also, how many people need this particular garment in this size. I am under five feet and weigh 96 lbs. Natalya does shorten it and sews horsehairs into the hem of the bell bottoms. Voila! It is officially a dance costume. The long-sleeved leotard will camouflage my body flaws. Long sleeves are better at my age. When you are nearing 80 years old, nothing is remotely smooth or perfect. Neither do I aspire to be perfect in the dance. I love the choreography, but the rhythm is challenging. We have a theme step with a little hop that gets repeated. Two days before the show, Alexey wants me to change the arms, because I don't straighten them to his satisfaction and don't turn my body enough. "No, no, I can't do it. I'll get my arm straighter and higher," I protest. I improve and Alexey says, "See, I just have to threaten you." There is a samba step that I beg him all along to take out. Good luck with that. Of course, it stays. It's called the "volta," for some strange reason. Maybe it's someone's name. Curse him, whoever he is. It always feels like a graceless limp. But Natalya gives me a few lessons and shows me a hip rotation that changes the look of the step dramatically. Yes, it is meant to look sexy! Hmm…. But it is too close to show time for me to be able to incorporate the "sexy" into my dance, so it will look half-baked for now. I am aware that a number of students do showy sambas. I feel embarrassed at my lack-luster efforts, because, after all, I have been taking lessons for ten years, and should do better. It is true that in my lessons we focus less on technique than on learning ever more complicated choreographies. The truth is that I like it that way. When this is over, I will start looking for music for the next one. Alexey tells me what he has in mind and I go hunting.

In the early years, he had me choose show tunes. I remember those dances as being less anxiety provoking, more fun. My favorite one was "Don't Tell Mama," when I got to wear a hot pink skirt and a bustier (borrowed from Genevieve). What fun! The last of that kind of dance was two years ago, to a Lena Horne song, "A Newfangled Tango." The audience loved it and it has the potential to be very sexy. But with Alexey, it's all business. Watch your arms, your footwork, your turn out, your hip motion and especially your head turns. And of course, it works, if you do it right. One woman came up to me after, threw her arms around me and said, "You are my hero." I think the homage belongs to Lena Horne and the clever lyrics, even though this dance, that moves from samba to tango to salsa to multiple turns, was, in fact, not so easy for me to learn.

The next dance I learn should be smooth and lyrical, he tells me, so I pick a Chopin *Ballade*. We agree that this kind of movement is most natural to me. It's my kind of movement and he tells me that I have moved to a higher level of dancing. Now samba is something else again and there is a lot of it in another one of my new dances. I am having foot problems. The lessons, the costumes, the event are all expensive. Still, I am compelled to dance more and more.

77. DANCING MILONGA

Emil reminds me we are to work on milonga today. I tell him that my energy is low but, "Okay, let's do it." I catch myself holding my breath during the warm-up dance. I think of Alexey's often repeated question, "Are you breathing?" Yes, my autonomic nervous system prevents me from turning blue and collapsing, but my anxiety shortens my breath and saps my energy. Emil observes as we dance the first milonga, "You say you have no energy, but you are light as a butterfly." Compliments, or "blarney," as Paul used to call it, stoke my engine. I do feel lighter. I think of the time ten years ago, when I was a beginner, and no one seemed to want to dance with me. At one social, two old men (probably no older than I am now), proclaimed after dancing a waltz with me that I was "light as a feather." One of them said: "We will call you Feather." The memory makes me smile. The playful milonga with its lively rhythm suits zany Emil. Today I find myself also almost effortlessly getting into its jazzy feel. I forget about being tired.

But I do tell Emil that I will be taking next month, July, off from my weekly hour tango lesson. With the travelling, it takes five hours out of my day. But I am sad. I don't really want to miss tango. After the music stops and I leave the studio and walk to the shuttle and I am dragging my feet, I feel dispirited and everything hurts. How long can I keep doing this?

It's Summer vacation time, so there are multiple groups of travelers at Grand Central, crowding around their guides. One tall grey bearded guy introduces himself: "Hello, my name is Larry." Another holds a red baseball cap aloft, instructing his group to look for it, to follow it, if lost in the crowd. It's many years since I have travelled with a group. I feel a bit envious of these people discovering Grand Central Station for the first time and bonding with strangers in following the red baseball cap. This station would be impressive, if you hadn't been there before. I still notice its grandeur, but mostly I am focused on making the 3:20 p.m. train, which is almost always to be found at the furthest away gate. Sometimes, like today, I am early, and I consider buying a coffee if the line isn't too long. In any case, no need to speed walk. Running is no longer in my repertoire. When I sit down in the train, I find I am freezing. Isn't there a power shortage? Why do they crank the air conditioner up so high? I scootch down in my seat, trying to keep warm. Off course this is a local and the 40-minute trip seems endless.

78. LOTS OF WAYS TO BE SAVED

It's my tango lesson in the city day. I am not motivated lately. I miss too many lessons. The trip by train gets harder. I'm getting older, or I am not in such a good mood today, but I like reading on the train. I have a paperback copy of Joan Didion's *Play It as It Lays* for this trip. I find a quiet spot and immerse myself in the novel and in Marya, who becomes more vivid the more she retreats from the world around her. The train ride is over too soon, and I have to leave her behind. I scramble down the stairs to the shuttle to Times Square. Hordes of people are streaming out in my direction. We, the next group of passengers, crowd in as best we can. I get a seat so I can carefully put away my senior MetroCard, zipper up my peacock-green down coat and fish my cozy grey mittens out of my backpack. People look beaten up by the weather, by the day, by life. Maybe it's just how I feel. Most everyone wears black. Someone at the end of the car is making music, mellow for once, on some kind of keyboard instrument. Everyone ignores him. Most people have their eyes glued to their electronic devices. A tall, light-skinned black man, in his seventies maybe, with deep lines etched into his face, enters the car, talking loudly to everyone. I think to myself, "Here's another psychotic person, released too soon from the hospital, who has gone off his meds". He sits directly opposite me, next to a middle-aged blond woman with a red beret. He starts talking to her as though he were resuming an ongoing conversation. He's not nasty or aggressive and the woman, initially tense, settles down and answers his conversational gambits. I am thinking that he might be manic but hasn't reached a dangerous stage. Last week a young man was cursing loudly, nonstop with allusion to it's or someone's being "hot." Everyone left the train as quickly as possible at Times Square. We've all learned to not make eye contact and the mentally ill and the homeless live unnoticed in a kind of anonymous Hell.

I feel an icy gust of air as I leave the train and I hear someone drumming across the street, a good rhythm on an improvised instrument. It's Broadway. On every block people are hawking their wares: tickets for a tourist bus, falafel, designer samples. There's a new upscale restaurant where a tuna sandwich costs $22. On the same block there's a cart offering halal chicken kebabs. As always there's the Mitzva Bus that announces the Meshiach. Someone asks, "Are you Jewish? Do you want a picture of the Rebbe?" I hurry past quickly. Yes, I am Jewish, but I don't want a picture of the Rebbe. Last week there was a man distributing pamphlets, offering salvation. Two blocks later there was a man carrying a sign saying, "Repent! Follow Jesus." Everyone is rushing off to their destination in couples, singly, in groups of three or four. A man takes a photo of his wife in front of a poster of the Statue of Liberty at a souvenir shop. Me, I am off to my tango lesson.

79. MAUDLIN

I get maudlin when I don't sleep enough. I am sad. When I don't sleep my defenses crumple and I cry. On the way to my writing group, I am crying. Here I go feeling sorry for myself, over-dramatizing. I haven't been able to dance the last few days. I catch myself almost writing "two years," when it's only been two days. I hurt too much, so I had to give up on Saturday's lesson. Has the time come that I will have to stop?

Recently, I have looked through journals from earlier years. That concern comes up repeatedly. I remember telling an instructor about my upcoming shoulder surgery and his saying,

"You look terrified." It wasn't about the surgery; it was about having to stop dancing.

It occurs to me that my dancing the last ten years was not the expected trajectory for my life. I was going to live a quiet married life. My children and grandchildren would live nearby. I would babysit a lot and would make lasagna for big family dinners. Well, I was married for 25 years, but then I got divorced. No one expected that, least of all me. Nothing turned out the way it was expected. Even the adventure of meeting Paul and our settling down together was not part of the likely scenario. Neither was his death from cancer after 15 years, nor again my plunging into a new life. My father liked everything to be under control. Nothing was under control. He was shocked to hear I hoped to meet someone else after my divorce. He looked at me and said "you??" None of it was in the cards. Certainly, my life being wrapped around dance was not part of the game.

My dance, even though seemingly out in the open, feels like a guilty secret, an out-of-control obsession that can be taken from me at any time. The ghost of my parents and their "evil eye" looked away long enough for it to evolve, for me to experience this joy. So, it is a secret but at the same time, I want everyone to come see me dance, to give me the seal of approval, to give me permission. Every time I have a new pain, I tell myself, "It's over. You have been found out. You are too old." And I ask myself, "What do I do now?" I chastise myself, tell myself to be grateful for the unexpected gift of these past years. But I am greedy and that's forbidden too. I want more. I know I don't deserve more. I have had more than my share, but it's never enough.

Why do you always say "maybe," tentative, on tender hooks, hooked into the past, into uncertainty, wobbly in your convictions? Dare to say, "yes, and now I choose." I say: rip through ambiguities, complexities to pure desire, flaming hot, crystal clear. Come out from the doubts of the diaspora, from the grey rooms, from the still, stale air of regret. Just say "Yes!"

80. AQUARIUS

During intermission at a flamenco show, Diana's boyfriend Rob and I end up discussing astrological signs. Neither one of us admits to believing in astrology, but we can't help being intrigued. He is mock outraged when I tell him that those born under the sign of Taurus, like himself, are stubborn. "But that's my daughter, Genevieve," I tell him. Besides, determined, diligent and loyal also apply. We get into the volatile Gemini. That's his ex-wife, my ex-husband, and an ex-boyfriend (lots of exes ... hmm…), but also my daughter, Julie. They all fit the profile, except of course, Julie, who is mostly charming and doesn't have the more distressing symptoms of Gemini-ism. Sadly, I am born under a dull sign: "Cancer: homebody, nurturing, somewhat dark at times." This profile says nothing of my excitement at watching this show. I get to see a disproportionate amount of this kind of dance, because my friend Juanita is a Flamenco dancer. I don't know much about it besides what I read in a cheesy romantic novel about passion and the necessity of being born a Gypsy to be authentic. I wish I remembered the title. It was really bad, but such fun.

In spite of the occasional forays to watch dance or films, I do seem to be a homebody. I don't travel much in the last 15 years. If Google were tracking me—and I am told it tracks everyone's movements—the robot or program or whatever is manning this enterprise would fall asleep. Mostly I make weekly trips to Manhattan, frequent trips to Ardsley and to Stew Leonard's (because they have fresh fish). Yawn! My Google searches might prove more intriguing. Now the Robot is confused. Why would I be looking for front tie shrugs in the morning and for Solzhenitsyn at night?

I did make it to Maine to visit Genevieve this month and there are several weather searches for that week and that location. The warnings that it would be cold and rainy were completely false alarms. Robots or programs or apps aren't supposed to mess up that way. Still, good surprises, such as mild Summer days in glacial Maine are most welcome. Order, logic, efficiency can be overrated. But what am I talking about? Chaos reigns! What about the four cars reserved in my name at the airport for the same day, the same time span, all Fords? If

Google maps is tracking me, it may be having me fly to Indonesia three times per year. That's not like a Cancerian. Maybe I am Aquarius instead. It is true that I used to fly to Chicago every six weeks to visit my Gemini boyfriend, now ex, of course. Did Google wonder? It is also true that, though I don't dance Flamenco, I can be entranced, watching the powerful Soledad Barrio and her troupe dancing *Antigone* in a smoky Church. The mix of Spanish and Greek can jolt you into another astrological sign, just like that.

81. BELGIUM: AT THE SEASHORE

People seem shocked when I tell them that I was a chubby child. In fact, I used to be embarrassed to be seen eating. A fat child should be ashamed to eat. To compound the issue, both my parents were fat-phobic, though my mother struggled her whole life towards the unattainable slim body.

But I did eat and there were special foods that I associate with what might have been our first family holiday at the seashore after the war. There we were, my parents and I and two other couples also with only children, celebrating our survival.

I can still taste a spicy tomato soup, served at the small hotel at which we stayed. There were also French fries, sold in a paper cone on the boardwalk. There was also talk of "rollmops," a kind of herring but that might have been a treat more appreciated by the adults.

These days I don't crave food except for chocolate, ice cream and oatmeal cookies. But the memory of those foods stays intertwined with the feel of the sand, the smell of suntan lotion and the sound of the crashing waves. I remember also my father cupping his hand under my chin to teach me to swim and his running after my rented child's bike to keep me from crashing. There are photos of me with long unruly brown hair and a too-small, blue, one-piece bathing suit. My parents had allowed me to invite a girlfriend to come along. She deserted me early on for more interesting company and to trade paper flowers with other children at the beach. I remember that some flowers were more valuable than others. I wanted to be part of that game. Was I? Who made them? Was it the children? But the most vivid memories were of the taste of soup, of food that I never remember craving afterwards. It belonged only to that Summer in Knocke, Belgium, post war.

82. SURPRISE CONTEST

Yesterday Miguel and I won third prize at a tango contest. We have always resisted Emil's invitations to compete, but here we are after all. Emil has a monthly Saturday night milonga, which I avoid these days, whenever I can resist his blandishments. It starts at 9:30 p.m. and it's on 35th Street between Sixth and Seventh Avenue, where it is almost impossible to park. But when I see Emil on Friday, he insists I come, sealing the deal, so he thinks, by telling me he is performing that night. I say, "What time?" He says, "For you, I will do it at 11:30 p.m." I know he's lying and anyway that's already pretty late. I won't be home until 1:30 a.m. This week I am in the city for tango Thursday, Friday, and now I agree to Saturday. Thursday is my weekly lesson with Miguel or on my own. Friday is another story altogether. It's for an event that Emil calls "Tango Elegante" with the idea that we older women are elegant. Flattery does get him a good part of the way! Besides the elegant idea, which actually doesn't do much for me, he tells me I am a legend, that he talks about me all the time, holds me up as an example, that the other "girls" (one of us is 83 years old) are dying to meet me. I know that this is nonsense, but I agree to come once a month and I have to admit that it's fun, even though no one at all is in awe of me. Of course, a dance teacher has to be a salesman and whatever else you can say about Emil, he is a good teacher and super as a partner.

I am still standing on Friday after the two-hour "Tango Elegante," and even Saturday morning, after my hour lesson with Alexey, so I don't cancel Saturday night's dancing at the milonga with Miguel, as I had thought I might do. I am not feeling all that well when I meet Miguel for coffee at "our diner," but I hope it will pass. Since Emil cut down on his milongas, we haven't been to the diner much and now most of the staff doesn't recognize us. We used to get a friendly greeting. One of the waiters even admonished Miguel, about often being late to meet me. I have learned to take a book to read, while I wait. He is on time tonight and I have miraculously found parking, a few blocks East. Not bad, except for feeling nauseous and for Miguel's seeming in low spirits. The conversation languishes and we make our way to the Ball and catch the last 15 minutes of Emil's lesson.

Around 11 p.m., Emil summons us urgently. He needs to talk to us. I am suspicious. What now? He tells us that several couples from New Jersey, Rockland County, and Connecticut didn't show up for the contest, even though they had paid the fee in advance. He needs us and some other innocent dancers, who just happened to show up for the milonga, to dance in the competition. As an added bonus, we don't have to pay the entry fee. It is all for free and we should just dance, the way we normally do, no jumps, no gancho, it's salon style. He looks me over and says, "You look good" and tells Miguel he looks good too. The first couple that he collared looks exceptionally good. The young woman is wearing an extremely tight short red skirt and extravagant jewelry. Miguel, who doesn't like the guy, thinks she's a call girl, not because of her outfit but because she is so attentive to her partner. I'm not convinced. I don't like the guy all that much myself, but maybe she is in love with him. Maybe that's not impossible. Miguel doesn't like him, because he tried to pick up his girlfriend, promising her the opportunity to be in a show with him. I don't like him because he avoids dancing with me, even at group lessons, where you change partners every few minutes. Someone pins a number on Miguel's back. We tell everyone, who will listen, that we were drafted against our will. Neither one of us will admit that we don't mind showing off that much. At least I don't really mind. Of course, it takes a while to get all this started. I am still feeling queasy and my head is reverberating with fatigue. We dance two songs. It feels as though we were relatively smooth and connected, with Miguel holding me tight. He tells me later that the embrace is solid because he doesn't want me to fall. Really? Have I ever fallen? It is after midnight and I put on my clumsy boots to head to my car. It's even past the time the coach turns into a pumpkin and I am done and undone. I see one of the judges, an attractive Latina woman in a sexy dance costume, in the ladies' room. She is going to perform. I tell her that I regret missing her performance, but that I must go home. She smiles at me and says, "No, no, you must stay for the prizes. You could be a champion." I decide I really can't walk out on her performance with Emil. She is dazzling and effortless, seeming to enjoy herself. I am still sitting in my clumsy boots with my coat on my lap, when they announce that Miguel and I have won third prize. I am embarrassed about my boots and want him to collect the trophy. He says that it's usually the woman who goes up. In the event we both go up to be applauded, me in my boots and trying to take off my jacket unobtrusively. We collect between us two trophies, a bottle of wine, a CD, a long-stemmed yellow rose, and a cupcake in a plastic container, which Miguel takes for a flower. Later I find out that we also earned three free admissions to Emil's milonga. That means we have to come, doesn't it? What's up for next time?

83. SAFE DEPOSIT BOX

The letter from the bank informs me that the Branch in Hartsdale is closing, that all clients must empty their safe deposit boxes. Mine has been in their custody at least 25 years. Is there enough material for a memoir? Perhaps! There's my birth certificate in German. There is also my certificate of citizenship with a photo. It's 1955 and I am a radiant 18-year-old. I have a vague memory of being asked some questions by an official. Was I sworn in? There are papers from my divorce lawyer, stating that the marital home is deeded to me: "The person of the first part, etc., ... My lavishly decorated marriage certificate, dated September Fifth, 1960, witnessed by a former friend of my young husband's and by Barbara (still my friend and almost as old as I am), has never made it into the safe. It is in a top drawer upstairs with diplomas, etc. It is inscribed with a fragment of The Song of Songs: "My beloved is mine." Shir Ha Shirim, as it is called in Hebrew, poetic and sensual, is one of my favorite books in the Bible; but now it is clear that no one ever belongs to anybody, nor should they. Well, that is politically correct, of course, but Martin and I both felt we belonged to each other, arms around each other, as protection from the callousness of the world, more or less anyway, and for many years.

What particularly moves me is a letter from my father. There is no year on the date, just 1/9. He writes: "Darling, it was nice talking to you, but I'm pretty much upset by your financial situation." The word "upset" sets off an immediate sense of alarm in me. He died 17 years ago and still his being "upset" leaves me momentarily uneasy. I spent my life dodging, avoiding, trying to placate both my parents. Of course, the "upset" was generated by his concern for me. Yet it feels as though it is my fault. My failure is implicit. Why doesn't his calling me "darling" remind me that I was loved? It has the same emotional valence to me as "sincerely yours," for instance. There's something wrong with my response. Does it go back to my being sent away at age five or is it the angry criticism, the silences, my omnipresent fear of being caught out, of saying the wrong thing?

In the rest of the letter, he gives a detailed account of the location of his safe deposit box, the phone numbers of his lawyers, accountants, etc. It is time to write a similar letter to my daughters. As to my financial situation at the time of the letter, I can't imagine what that might have been about. I never experienced a financial panic, not for long anyway. My father kept me safe, came to the rescue. His expressions of love often took the form of giving money, including a yearly stipend. Once, in a moment of crisis, he did tell me he loved me and, also later when he had dementia in his nineties. Did he recognize me? He didn't understand me or see me as a separate person, but he loved his daughter fiercely.

So many years, the three of us, my father, my mother and I lived with the sound of bitter silence in the house, punctuated by my father's angry outbursts. But it wasn't always so. It's what I remember with disappointment, sadness for all of us. There are also recollections of stories about the war and lighter fare, jokes, childhood memories that reach as far back as 1915, to a different kind of life. I try to imagine my father as a boy walking to school in the early morning, while it was still dark, a very long walk. So many details about his life are now gone forever. I save the letter. It now makes me feel tender towards him, my resentment forgotten. A long life is complicated, full of mystery and compromise!

84. TANGO ELEGANTE ENCORE

I have promised Emil that I would come to his Friday evening "Tango Elegante," where I and three other women, for a price, get to dance with him and some other man. The latter would be the mystery guest. He never seems to know beforehand which male dancer he can cajole into getting there. Emil was extremely cross with me when I told him I wasn't coming the previous Friday because the trains were still in slow down mode after a fire under the tracks in Harlem. I have to go this week, no matter the condition of my feet. Well, the train is easy if I find parking not too far away from the station. Also, the shuttle always teems with interesting people, unexpected sights. Today a young woman with a headscarf, wearing a green shirt that says, "Chic and Pretty," makes her way purposefully through the crowd. I sit next to a young man with bulging biceps covered in tattoos. He's solid looking, about 5'7' and wears his gleaming black hair in a chignon, under a baseball cap. I wonder about his story. Most people are glued to their devices, but others have conversations. Some of the languages I recognize, Spanish, French, German, Hebrew. I guess at Arabic and at Slavic languages. Today a slim young blonde woman in a black mini dress offers me a seat. I accept gratefully My first sight as I step outside the subway on to Times Square is of a half-naked man, displaying rolls of fat, sitting on a crate, playing a drum with flippers, clearly an unfortunate birth defect. Still, he can make music without arms.

It was so hot at home. Now that I am in New York City, it's cloudy, cool, if somewhat humid. I have plenty of time, so I stroll, taking in the sights. I cross the street to find a coffee shop. It's a totally different world on this side of Broadway. Tables and chairs line the street. There are multiple Urban Space kiosks selling anything from tacos and hot dogs to croissants. My coffee is too hot to drink, and I decide to carry it with me to the studio, so I can sip it intermittently. My feet still hurt, but I am enjoying my leisurely walk.

This week, it is a bonanza. There is only one other woman, besides myself and I get to dance a lot with Emil. He does seem to give the "other woman," Jan, more dances and I boldly step up and tell him: "My turn, Emil." He obliges and seems to enjoy the dances. He smiles impishly and picks me up off the floor and twirls me around in a high sentada. I like his madcap energy. I am lucky that today he doesn't turn me upside down, that he remembers that I might not be dressed appropriately for this feat. Jan, a woman probably in her late 70s or early 80s wears a long purple print chiffon skirt with black leggings and a black leotard and heeled black boots. She is the epitome of Bohemian chic. She has a rapturous expression on her face and closes her eyes when she dances with Emil. During one of the dances, Emil brings up the Stage Tango class. I say my rehearsed speech, "I can't do it this time, Emil. Please, don't give me a hard time." He is pacified for the moment. I can just keep on postponing going to the Friday night Tango Elegante. I did say "once a month," and maybe I can get away with doing it every two months. It may work. No one believes that I can resist his blandishments; everyone thinks that I will cave in. Tonight, he does ply us with cherries, strawberries, chocolates, champagne and wine. Yes, of course, we are paying for the strawberries, but still, they make a good impression. I am so easily manipulated and surprisingly my feet hurt less at the end of two hours.

85. LOST

My mind suddenly goes blank. That often happens at rehearsals. I don't know where I am, what dance I am doing. My mind wanders; I don't know where it goes even, but I have lost the plot. Alexey picks up vagueness immediately. He says, "Na-omi, stay with me. Stay connected." Yesterday, he says, "You look lost."

Still today, he tells me, I was able to stay focused enough to rehearse all of my eight dances (I hadn't noticed). I will probably perform all of them at the Showcase at the end of January. I am exhausted by the effort of concentrating for a 45-minute lesson.

On the other hand, I am told, it takes much energy to keep distracted. For instance, Martha Stewart's endless inventory of what to pack for a trip sounds labor intensive, but it does guarantee that she will be able to avoid even ten minutes of reflection. I recognize the syndrome. As soon as I enter my empty house, I turn on the radio, play a CD, turn on the TV, play a movie, pick up the telephone, anything to avoid the oppressive silence. The sound is turned off on my dreams of being lost, having forgotten the address, not being able to dial the phone. So, I must dance!! Yes, Pina Bausch: "Dance, dance or we are lost."

86. SATURDAY MILONGA

The weekend is going to be complicated. Miguel says to me, "Don't let yourself be bullied." He's right of course but it takes just subtle pressure to get me to do things I don't want to do. I have my tango lesson with Emil this Thursday. He's mellow, reviewing basics with me. At the end of the lesson, he plays a lovely Astor Piazzollo piece and we flow along to the music. He asks then whether I am coming to his monthly Saturday night milonga. I risk his ire (at least it's the end of the lesson) and say "No," but immediately undo the insult by promising to come to his new Friday milonga. I tell myself that I will take public transportation and that it won't be so bad. Oh no, I realize suddenly, it's the next day and I haven't figured out the bus route to this new venue.

It turns out that Friday is rainy and cold, and the wind is howling. Beware of rash promises! I would get soaked, taking the train, the bus and then walking, and I would get home even later than for the usual Saturday fiasco. Diana, who doesn't get to dance often enough, says she would like to go on Saturday, and she would drive. She won't go by herself and of course, not heeding Miguel's good advice, I feel I owe Emil, that I have to show up this weekend, since I didn't keep my promise about Friday. I get all gussied up with short skirt, lacy top with flowing sleeves and my new Michal Negrin choker (I have to wear it. I bid for it on eBay). I do notice, when I go dancing, that women in short skirts get asked more often, even if they are over 50 years old, like me (try over 79 years old, almost 80? We will see). At least I get to do ballroom with Miguel on Sunday and what could be better?

In tango, the tradition is for the man to lock eyes with you if he's asking you to dance and it's for a group of tangos, called a *tanda*, usually three or four. Usually I meet Miguel, but even when assured of a good partner, I tend to avoid the Saturday night milonga. I dread the traffic midtown with everyone beeping at you as you drive around the congested blocks, looking for the impossible dream, a legal parking spot. The dancing starts at ten p.m. I don't like getting home a two a.m. and feeling miserable the whole next day.

Diana gets here late, but there is no traffic. I love being the passenger and am in good spirits. After driving around, maybe a half hour, we find parking right in front of the studio. Unbelievable! Sadly, there is homeless man swaddled in dirty rags, sleeping to the right of the door to the building. We walk in to find Emil, Marie and a youngish blonde man standing in the lobby, involved in conversation. Emil looks despondent. There is a major glitch! The floor to that night's social is locked and therefore the elevator won't go there and there is no access through the stairs. The youngish man explains the problem, makes calls, considers alternatives. The elevator repairman is not likely to save the night. It will have to wait till morning. He jokes that, having gotten parking, we should stay overnight. He commiserates, saying, "Here you are looking beautiful, all decked out." Diana and I take a break at a local eatery. When we come back more dancers have assembled in the lobby. I see Thomas, a young, tall black man, a musician in civilian life and everyone's favorite. There's Madeline, a high energy tango dancer and lawyer. She has just written a book about tango news and gossip, which she is enthusiastically hawking. I am intrigued, but Diana and I don't have enough cash.   More people arrive. The pace takes on the atmosphere of a non-threatening bomb shelter. Emil feels responsible, He wants to stay until the repairman arrive. All night? This time it is not his fault. I am not disappointed. I don't have to suffer the humiliation of not being asked to dance and there is ballroom with Miguel tomorrow. We consider going to another milonga, Mala Leche, a few blocks away. In the end Diana prefers going home, rather than dealing with a roomful of strangers. We head home. It's still late when I get to sleep, but not one a.m. I wake up from strange dreams and thoughts. I imagine the elevators clanging, banging up and down in a jerky cha cha. I see the homeless man pulling off his rags and walking in resplendent in clean clothes. Emil has turned on his computer and tango music plays in the lobby and filters out into the street. I am dancing with Thomas in my Uggs. What could be better? And we didn't even pay an entrance fee.

87. GOODBYE MR. CHIPS

My daughter Genevieve writes in an e-mail, "The ponies down the road are sweet and I am thinking of baking bread." That night I watch *Goodbye Mr. Chips* on Turner Classic Movies. Am I hopelessly sentimental to love this old film? I am caught in a time warp.

Young Mr. Chippins arrives at the turn of the century, some time before World War One, to teach at a boys' boarding school. It is his first teaching assignment. He is awkward and timid. It is all so innocent. Yes, I know the film doesn't deal with the hidden darker aspects that exist always: bullying, beatings, rejecting, abusive parents, hidebound, unfeeling bureaucracy. But still, I want to immerse myself, believe in this world of decency and kindness. There is also the pivotal scene in which Mr. Chippins, with much encouragement from his friends, dances a Viennese Waltz at a ball with the woman he marries. She fills his life with warmth and light.

The next night I watch *The Circle*, based on the novel by Dave Eggers, who is a very clever man. You could call it science fiction, but it feels like a probable scenario. The Circle is a cult which demands total transparency from its employees. Everyone is wired to be in constant communication with the rest of the Community. Secrets are lies. Privacy is an offense. So, it's Facebook, writ large and no longer voluntary.

In my car, I am listening to Dan Brown's book *Origins*. The protagonist, who appears in all of Brown's novels, is a Symbologist, who grapples with the interface between religion and science. The plot revolves around the attempt of a religious community to suppress a renowned Futurist's predictions about where we, as the human race, are going and also where we come from: "the laws of gravity versus Genesis." His conclusion that the human race will meld with technology by 2050 feels prescient. That this will lead to eradicating hunger and disease, cleaning up pollution, the abolition of war, a general improvement of the world, seems Utopian. Unfortunately, as long as human beings maintain control, the earth will be ravaged, the helpless and the poor will be mowed down. What about Artificial Intelligence? Potentially it could achieve great progress. But what about the moral compass? Spoiler: The all-knowing computer created by the Futurist arranges several murders to preserve his master's message. It wasn't specifically programmed not to do this. What about kindness, compassion, Art? I would like to believe in Mr. Chips and in Mr. Smith, who goes to Washington. So, often, I lull myself into fantasy watching old movies.

Yes, maybe my daughter will bake bread and maybe will feed the ponies and she will be happy in the sunshine, most of the time, I hope. But none of it will be simple. None of it can be simple.

88. TANGO BLUES

The street looks washed clean this morning, after all the rain that pelted the neighborhood last night, but a pigeon has besmirched the passenger side window of my car. It's ugly, mars my desire for a new day, all angst dissipated, with the pale morning sun, promising a clearer mind.

Nothing terrible has happened in my life and yet both Friday and Saturday night, or I should say more accurately early mornings, three a.m. to five a.m., I find myself munching crackers and Tylenol and wondering why the night is so long when you can't sleep. It's absurd, but I am ruminating over tango and tango partners. Upon seeing an acquaintance at a milonga this weekend I tell her, in my discouragement, that I feel like giving up tango. She says, "That would be too bad, because you are an inspiration." When people tell me that kind of thing, I suspect it is because of my age, like being amazed at a dog walking on it hind legs. I give her the thumbs down signal.

Tango is the partner dance, *par excellence,* but I can't seem to follow my partner. It used to feel smooth, tango with Miguel, or maybe my memory fails me; maybe there were always too many ruts in the road, and me stumbling off the wrong foot. You take the smooth passages, the moments of elegance for granted.

This Friday night I agree to dance with Emil. I take the train and then the shuttle to Times Square to a milonga on 46th Street. I haven't been at the heart of the City for a while. On the train, a young Black woman gets in with a baby in a carrier and a large red suitcase. She asks me how to get to a bus to take her back to D.C., where she has been living the last seven years. She tells me she originally came from the Central Republic of Africa. She tells me how hard it is to take care of a little one, how he always has to come first. I commiserate, but I am happy to have a conversation. Most train passengers these days are immersed in their electronic devices and not available for any interactions with a stranger, or even a friend.

On the street the glitz and excitement of Times Square washes over me. Theoretically, I reject the huge billboards, the garish store fronts, the boorishness of big Capitalism. Yet the festive atmosphere, the mix of different languages, the hopefulness of the crowd makes me feel lighter. I am suddenly optimistic about the evening.

It is not yet five p.m., my meeting time with Emil, but people are already moving around the floor at the milonga. I am wearing klutzy sneakers and hurry to change into my low-heeled dance shoes. Ah, if only I could wear those striking four-inch heeled tango shoes! But I am wearing a short skirt and immediately a swarthy, possibly middle-aged man asks me to dance. He is not bad and turns out to be one of Emil's students. Emil agrees with my verdict more or less, says he's not too good. Well, the glass half empty. The next dancer, a stocky man I have danced with before. This is much better. He holds me close and at least for this *tanda* we feel connected. I say to him, "That was nice." He responds with emphasis, "That was *very* nice." I think to myself that the secret is actually enjoying the tango with a particular person. That is not a brilliant observation, but it leads me to think that both Miguel and I are too worried about getting the technique right. It is definitely true for me. He says that I lose my balance and pull him off center, so that he hurts his knee. Not good! The following week, at a milonga, I will observe to him that the young couple in the middle of the floor, who have no clue about tango, are having a better time than anybody else. He will say, "That is the way it's supposed to be. You are supposed to enjoy dancing." But of course, sometimes we don't.

When Emil arrives, he is immediately engrossed in his phone and in greeting his students. We have contracted to dance for an hour. He lets me know right away that he resents dancing every dance. He announces that Miguel's injuries are due to my insisting on dancing every dance. He tells me that Bella, who is his next student, doesn't like every song and wants to sit out some of them. When I say that I like to dance every dance, he retorts: "No, you just want to be sure you get your money's worth." And with that I am angry and want the hour to be over and to take any excuse to not dance with him. I usually follow Emil well, but today, I start making mistakes. In response, he says, "Aha, now I see what you are doing to Miguel!" That's when I decide, at least for this week, that tango is not for me.

When the hour is up, I leave instantaneously. The street has lost its luster and I look for a pharmacy to buy Tylenol, because the tendonitis on my foot has flared up. At our next lesson, Emil tells me how fabulous I am and works on some basic technique with me. I didn't want to go, but it was alright, because after all I am still "fabulous." So intermittently I will continue with tango, for now.

The next day, I again take the train downtown to dance at a milonga. Today instead of the cross-town bus, I take a subway that is supposed to land me near the studio on Seventh Avenue, within an easy walk to the studio. Instead, I find myself on Fifth Avenue. It's around Christmas, and it's all lit up and my feet don't really hurt that much. I see a man standing on the sidewalk with a cat on his head. He calls out to a little girl, sitting on her father's shoulders, "Hello, beautiful girl." I don't know which way is North or West, but passersby don't laugh at me when I ask. When I get to Sixth Avenue, I see a *Pret a Manger*. I am early and to kill some time, I go in and browse. It all seems very expensive and I opt for a cup of coffee. I am going to read my book, *The Days of Abandonment*, by Elena Ferrante. It's rather gloomy fare but the coffee is strong and just the way I like it. When I go to pay, the clerk tells me, "It's on the house." I can hardly believe it. After all, it's New York City. Christmas good cheer?

Then on to the milonga, to a different world. Miguel arrives a few minutes after me, looking dapper in a dark pin-striped suit. Before joining me, he has a too-long, earnest conversation with a young Asian woman, Ashley. His young women friends are a thorn in my side, but after all, for the next few hours he is mine. No gypsy music tonight, but it is still rich and sensual. I let myself imagine we are lovers. We dance in close embrace and do a lot of sexy leg wraps and ganchos. My tango teacher, Emil, teaching ganchos, urges, "higher on the thigh, let your leg brush his thigh." We both laugh when I look at him quizzically, but "higher on the thigh" it is. I wonder whether Miguel is totally immune to the sexual charge of it all. But never mind; for now, we are "lovers." When he touches my arm going into the embrace, it's a caress. I feel his breath, when he whispers in my ear. He is dancing with someone else after me, so I miss his walking me to the subway and the chaste kiss on the lips we share when we part.

89. JUST A GIGOLO?

Sometimes at socials, I am aware that people are watching Miguel and me. He is an elegant dancer and I'm not bad, probably pass for his student. Once a woman enthusing about how well we dance, invited us to a private social. Tonight, there is a man following me with his eyes. He gives me a tentative wave. As I am getting ready to leave, he accosts me as I walk by. He says: "You look very sensuous. You should wear a long black, strapless evening gown. Black suits you." How does he know? Perhaps he has watched me on another occasion. We exchange some chit chat. Surrounded by the noise of the dance floor, I almost miss the Irish accent. His name is Thomas and he is leaving for Ireland tomorrow. When I again pass where he is sitting, he asks me if I have a lover and suggests I sit with him a while. There is little doubt about his intentions. It is flattering to me to be noticed, but it is just as well that Miguel and I are on our way out together. His boldness unnerves me a bit. It feels a bit sinister when I think about it later. Is he a gigolo? No, he doesn't seem the type. He seems to be an ordinary man, interested in a one-night stand. He is slender, of no particular age, fair skinned with a pronounced snub nose, wearing jeans and a blue shirt. My encounter with gigolos has been limited to messages from drop-dead gorgeous, very young men on the dating site: "Seniors Meet." Though he is not in his dotage, this man isn't a stunning young buck. Could I still be attractive in a certain light?

90. ZINC BAR

I dream that my house opens up into large rooms that I have never seen. One bedroom has a king-sized bed, covered in a red satin bedspread. It's round or oval. I'm not sure how to describe it. I guess it's like in a Hollywood movie. Maybe there are mirrors on the ceiling! Miguel is in one of the smaller rooms, or is it a shower, because I ask him if he needs a clean towel.

For once, it seems to be a positive dream! This implies that my life is opening up, that I am discovering hidden reserves in myself. Some days, life does seem richer, stranger. But then, my other selves complain that I am alone, aimless, that maybe I don't have much longer to live.

Last night, sitting on the train, on my way downtown, it occurs to me that a different part of myself should have shown up for this adventure. I have agreed to meet my tango teacher, Emil, at the Zinc Bar on West Third street. I am angry at myself for having, as usual, caved in to his demands. Yes, of course it's a good idea to dance with him socially, at least once, before the show we are doing together in three weeks. But the dancing starts at nine p.m. and by train it takes me two hours to get there. He wants me to do two hours, but I insist on one hour (half the cost, of course). I will get home after midnight. I am anxious about which subway to take after the shuttle. The best part of the evening, I think on the way down, is reading *Night of the Iguana* on the train. What pleasure!

Now another self would be thrilled, curious about the few people on the train, the subway and on the street on a rainy Sunday night and the prospect of tango with Emil. What a wet blanket I am tonight! So, what if the wind is whipping up at the train station in Hartsdale. She, this other self, wouldn't be alarmed at the endless maze of the subway, the long descent of the escalator into the bowels of the Earth. Am I on the right route? It seems improbable. Some people travel to exotic places, discover mysterious secrets, flirt with danger for the sake of adventure. You could argue that New York subways are hardly a sought-after destination. Still, I am annoyed with my kvetchy self for agreeing to go and then seeing everything through a haze of anxiety.

Then, I am dancing with Emil on a dimly lit dance floor to live music, a piano, a bass and a large harmonica. How strange to be here! What thrilling music! People are sitting at small tables, in a semicircle, around the dance floor, watching us. Ladies at some of the tables want Emil to dance with them. He announces portentously that he only dances with his students. They would have to take private lessons with him first. I am the lucky tango dancer tonight, as long as I don't consider the trip home.

91. TANGO PARTY

"What is your official title?" I ask. She says she is Emil's assistant and she helps him, because, "he's a good person." Later in the evening, it becomes clear that she is the current "tango wife." I remember years ago, a lovely woman named Susan would bring Emil's clean laundry to class. The exchange rate, I think, was free group lessons and milongas.

Tonight, Emil is having a barbecue with lots of food and wine, on the rooftop of his apartment. He does this several times a year, but it's my first time. I know, intuitively, not to come early. I know it would involve cutting up vegetables, putting out fruits and chips and following our host's contradictory orders. The tango wives are busy setting up the party when I get there. My friend, Diana, who talked me into coming, is also working. Later, she is dubbed the "tango mistress," because she mostly has fun. Gina, wife number one, who introduces herself as the "assistant," suggests I could be the "tango mother." Thanks for reminding me that I am the oldest person here. I decline to join the family. This isn't nearly as sordid as the Manson Family, but as the evening goes on the place fills up with mostly women, maybe 15 of us, and three men. The atmosphere is festive, friendly, and I relax on the roof, having avoided doing any work.

I had told Alexey about the event and he had warned, "It will be a walk-up and he'll live on the tenth floor." Getting lost in the neighborhood, arriving there perhaps still a bit too early is interesting. It is in Chinatown and has shops that would be fun to revisit, such as an Asian Clothing Vintage Store and lots of places selling Chinese herbs and tea. When I get to the address, I ring the bell and Diana comes down to let me in. I chuckle as I hoist myself up three flights of very steep stairs, hanging on to the banister. Tangos, lifts and drops I can do, but stairs are a challenge. And there is also the problem of getting back down the stairs, but I postpone thinking about that.

The small apartment is neat, and we are told to take off our shoes. In the hallway there are four shelves of men's shoes. Emil is fastidious. He likes to dress well. But the poster of a scantily dressed model's derriere on his refrigerator door raises eyebrows. I think that even the tango wives don't approve. There are some erotic drawings in his bedroom, but they are tasteful, even beautiful. Mostly we are in the living room, with the windows opened, and the weather is still balmy for September. Emil is on his best behavior, basking in the presence of his harem. I drink wine and sway to the music with my new inebriated friends.

92. LATE-LIFE CRISIS

It's the week after my 82nd birthday. All the dear people in my life call and wish me well. The day itself feels pleasant, even productive. But, is it time for me to read the books about facing your mortality that hide in the far corner of my bookshelf? It doesn't feel real just yet, that I must die. Perhaps that will change if I become ill. Maybe I will be one of the lucky ones who slips away quietly, finally tired and sated with life. For now, it occurs to me that I am having a "late-life crisis."

The mid-life crisis was co-opted by my ex-husband and so many others, mainly men. It explains everything: divorce, affairs with people of the opposite sex to your present partner, a trek up the Pyrenees, a shiny new motorcycle. My most dramatic gesture, when I get divorced at mid-life is to buy a tent, which I use maybe three times before eventually giving it away. Really, I always am much too well behaved, boring, I guess.

So, what is it to be now? First, does it need to be established that old people are capable of having such a crisis? No one writes about it. Does that matter? When you are in your eighties, you might not want a shiny new sports car. A chauffeur would be very nice indeed, thank you very much.

At various times in my life there are regrets about not being more successful in my career, not earning money, about not doing research and writing. I tell myself that I made my peace with all that, that it was all an inevitable given, that looking backwards doesn't change anything.

Regrets get touched off for me while watching movies and TV shows about close-knit groups of people, extended families in a way, but peopled by kindred souls, not blood ties. There have been loves and soul mates in my life. Of course, I want more. Is there someone out there who likes Iris Murdoch, someone who likes old movies, someone who would dance with me for hours? I am entranced by stories about large families, about twins and even about clones. But didn't I say, "not blood ties?"

Have you watched the series based on Armistead Maupin's *New York Stories*? The one that grips me is the one in which the old woman Anna Madrigal, played by Olympia Dukakis, celebrates her 90th birthday. I identify with the character played by Laura Linney, who returns for the huge party, after living in a straight "normal" world for many years. It feels like a homecoming for her. She looks as though she doesn't belong, but her heart is with the many lost, eccentric people who have become Anna Madrigal's surrogate children and grandchildren through the years. I am fascinated by the wildness, the love, the sorrow, the raw emotions of the people in this community. My life has been far too tame. Yet there isn't much I regret. Perhaps the desire is to have lived another more dramatic, more emotional parallel life, with many lovers and artistic fulfillment as well, and of course those many soul mates! That's not asking too much, is it? Of course, it's ridiculous to want everything. Still, I do wish I could have been more daring, more willing to take a larger bite of life.

93. RELICS OF THE PAST

The boxes of my parents' photos and papers have been sitting in the small bedroom upstairs for years, ever since my mother died, seven years ago. I did, on several occasions, make an effort to go through them to see what could be discarded, but with little progress. This month, my friend is in the process of packing up her belongings in order to move. I am told, in confidence, with a sigh of exasperation that she doesn't want to let go of any of her "treasures," and that, in short, she is a "hoarder."

I am galvanized into action, albeit briefly. No one is going to call me a "hoarder." My house is "lived in," has been called pleasantly "cluttered," but there are open spaces. You can walk from one room to another, without stumbling on unexpected obstacles, though there is the danger of the occasional mislaid shoe in your path.

So, with a few extra hours at my disposal, on a snowy day, it's time to tackle the boxes. My first find stops me in my tracks; my father's obituary from 2002, so matter of fact; date of birth, death, holocaust survivor, in medical practice for fifty years, married to my mother for sixty-five years. Never mind everything that is left out: a life, a person. Still, you can't throw this out. Among the many photographs, there are also yellowed newspaper clippings announcing the death of my paternal grandparents: Simon Silverstein, then Meta Silverstein, born Kolath. There is nothing for my mother. That was down to me. Did I not send an announcement to the local paper? Probably I did, but where is it?

Going through the photographs, I ruthlessly throw away the ones of flowers and buildings, of people with their heads cut off, the ones too faded to recognize with old eyes, the ones of people I don't know and also of my mother's best friend whom I detested. There are voluminous piles of letters on air mail paper, many in German, some in French. The ones from my father's lawyer,

Herr Meyerhoff, get tossed. But then there are my father's letters about his war experiences, his certificates of completion of his medical studies, letters of recommendation, his letter thanking the man who gave us the affidavit to come to this country, who made it possible for us to start a new life in this country. There are even old report cards. He was an average student. I find myself strangely moved reading a letter from another physician, saying my father performed his work, conscientiously and with devotion. Yes, "devouement." That would have been true for him. There's a plastic sign with black lettering that spells out: "Dr. Friederich Silverstein, MD." Why does it feel wrong to throw that away? I have no use for it, but I can't throw it out. It was his identity.

94. MISSED THE BUS

I am hoping to make it to the Madison Avenue bus, in time to catch the 4:31 train back to Hartsdale. My tango lesson has been moved to 31st Street between Fifth Avenue and Broadway. It's a new itinerary for me and I am momentarily disoriented, not realizing that the Fifth Avenue bus goes in the wrong direction. I accelerate my pace, as I see buses lumbering up the Avenue in the distance. Then my klutzy UGGs get in the way. I trip and crash land on the sidewalk and, of course, miss the bus. My arthritic knees challenge my getting off the ground in any normal way. I manage a downward dog, stepping gradually closer to my hands and, voila, I am upright, just slightly bruised. Two weeks later, I am still not sure which bus to head for, albeit, more cautiously after my headlong dive on to the concrete.

Yes, I am back to tango in New York City after a three months break. It took three weeks for my toe to heal, but I needed some time off from Emil. When I return, I am actually glad to see him? The "glam" studio in which he used to teach has closed down; no more dazzling professional dancers, reflected in the large wrap-around mirrors to intimidate me. We are now at the somewhat shabby Pierre Dulaine Studio. There are posters of his three films on the wall: "Mad Hot Ballroom," "Take the Lead," and "Dancing in Jaffa," in which he starred. So, when he comes into the studio, I recognize him instantly. I don't usually recognize anyone famous, let alone talk to them, but I tell him that I loved all three films. He blows me a kiss.

Aside from Paul Dulaine's presence, this new venue is undistinguished. There is a Wine and Chocolate Bar, practically next door, and that intrigues me. I heard the person at the reception desk discuss truffles with strawberries. Hmm.

The trip to the studio, via the Fifth Avenue bus can be interesting too. It's a less than five minutes ride, but you can learn a lot in that time. One day, a sandy haired, average-looking, middle-aged man greets me, as I sit down, with the comment, "You shouldn't fall after the age of forty." That sounds like sensible advice. Sure enough, his wrist is taped up. He fell down an elevator shaft and tore his meniscus. He doesn't give me much time to commiserate before launching into this story: "When I was a kid on a bus to Long Island, the driver had a nervous breakdown. He refused to let anyone out of the bus and told us we were going to Cuba." I was so amused by this story and really, I only had two minutes before being allowed off this bus, that I failed to ask him how it all ended. Did someone hijack the bus, talk down the driver? Was the driver a rapid cycler and his mania gave way to depression and he simply slumped in the driver's seat, having given up the plan? I tell this story to a writer friend and suggest she make up the ending. She likes the idea of having the passengers be a group of women who are on their way to the Women's March in Washington. What about a backstory for each passenger? Of course, the bus driver's imagined history may not be the most colorful of all. Still, you can wonder: Was he Cuban? Did he lose his job, his wife, his girlfriend, his boyfriend? Are his children disrespectful or in trouble? Was he just discharged from a psychiatric Hospital? Did he go off his lithium? What's up with the storyteller?

95. SWEETIE

On my way downtown, at the train station, the meter maid says, "No, honey. I don't have any change. Try the meter." What meter? I think. I am not observant and notice the new Muni meter only several weeks later, when I try to use it and it doesn't work. I am going to miss my train, unless I get creative about this parking issue very quickly. Maybe I should just risk getting a ticket. Sometimes, you can get lucky.

I am 82-years old and five-feet tall and am often called "sweetie" or "honey". I know it's patronizing and that I should be annoyed, but sometimes it just feels affectionate. Am I so starved for affection that anything will do? What I really loathe is being called "cute". I didn't even like it when I was young, when it could also have been, "Hey, Babe," or catcalls.

They tell you to age gracefully and leave the things of youth behind. "Sweetie" and "honey" aside, I don't feel old. Maybe that's why I experience the meter maid and shop keepers as being merely friendly. I do think often about when I am going to have to stop dancing. In some abstract way, I wonder how and when I am going to die. At best, I have lived three quarters of a long-life span. In some ways, the last decade has been the best so far. So, you can call me "sweetie" anytime.

96. BEING JOYOUS

I was complaining to Miguel on the phone this week, about being tired much of the time. A comment from a 15-year-old girl comes to mind: "When people say they're tired, it means they are sad." It is true that my defenses crumple when I don't sleep enough and really, I am sad. Miguel said, "Remember you must do everything with joy." It would be easy to scoff at this, but I decided to take it seriously, reminding myself several times a day, "Do it with joy." It has been a gloomy time. My feelings about thousands of immigrant children being separated from their parents at the Border fills me with sorrow and hopeless fury.

Alexey, aware of my mood, keeps telling me, "Keep your head up. Tall and Proud. You are drooping. It makes your turns more difficult." My new choreography, to the Queen Latifah song in *Chicago*, has so many turns, that Alexey, who has set me this challenge, says that he would like to count them some time. But I have been moving without zest, drifting off, complaining about the awkwardness of dancing in heels. Yes, I know that I have to keep my head up, spot when I turn, keep my feet under my body, so take small controlled steps and of course, "don't rush, listen to the music and count and count." It does worry me sometimes that the audience will see my lips moving, when I count. For Alexey counting is a *sine qua non*. He sees and hears everything, particularly mistakes, or so it seems right now. I hear his warning voice: "Na-omi, don't be creative." But trying to be joyous changed everything, though my turns hadn't improved that much.

Today there was a memorial service for the mother of one of my friends. It took place at a Church, not a natural environment for me and also not a joyous occasion, though the eulogy was inspiring. My sciatica kicked in and I spent most of the service standing, leaning against a post. It did cross my mind that the deceased was only five years older than I.

Early rising today leaves me sleepy and yesterday's good intentions have already dissipated. I regret having already finished a wonderfully quirky novel: *Old Filth*, and not having a ready replacement. There are hundreds of books in my house. How is it that none of them seem appealing? I start reading a novel in Spanish, but today at least it feels way too difficult. My Spanish remains rudimentary. There are three more hours until my scheduled dance lesson and it is essential to cultivate an upbeat mood, in which my shoes don't hurt, and my turns are sharp and under control. I have already tried chocolate, but it probably won't do the trick. Maybe another conversation with Miguel will help. Still, it's not really o.k. to call him every day for inspiration. Sometimes, rehearsals don't go so well, but at least the repetition of the choreographies is useful, if not joyous. So, sometimes you have to settle for whatever is possible.

97. WINE AND CHOCOLATE BAR

On Thursday, I finally have lunch at the Wine and Chocolate Bar, two doors down from the Pierre Dulaine Studio, where I take my tango lessons these days. Right next door, there is a store displaying exceptionally ugly costume jewelry. It may look cheap, but since there are no prices in the window, it stands to reason that it is expensive. There are workmen loading carts into the freight entrance of the building and then there is the bar, with a prix fixe lunch at $10.95.

I am intrigued by the idea of truffles for lunch though, maybe because I am not supposed to eat chocolate. I have had the fantasy of a cozy *tête à tête* with a lover there. Well, there is nothing wrong with having a fantasy, is there? I am meeting my friend, Karen, who is not my lover, after my tango lesson and we will try out the place.

I have a satisfying lesson with Emil, just me today, as Miguel's knee is swollen. We are working on Vals. Dancing Vals with Emil feels like flying, but the technique, the angles are difficult to master when you break down the dance.

Karen and I were friends when our children, Genevieve and Lola, were three years old, over 50 years ago. She is a tall woman with a winning smile. I think of her as a brunette, but of course her hair is white now. It's odd how the image of her younger self persists for me. Today I notice that she looks tired, that she has fine wrinkles on her face, but her smile hasn't changed. We still like to talk. She reminds me of a time when her ex-husband, the villainous Manfred, kidnapped Lola and she pursued them to the Canadian border and managed to reclaim her with the help of the Canadian Mounties. Mannie, as she calls him, has shown no interest in his daughter in the ensuing years. She tells me that I lent her money at that time. I don't remember this part.

Here we are, perched on stools at the back of a bar after my tango lesson, so many years later. The waitress tells us we should try their special, a "chocolate martini." Ugh!! They do bring us complimentary cups of sangria and a dish of what seem to be nuts but turns out to be spiced crackers that burn your tongue. I discreetly tear off a piece of a navy-blue napkin, to dispose of the radioactive cracker. I order humus and Karen orders a yogurt-based Middle Eastern dip. My dish is inedible. We should have proceeded immediately to the chocolate truffle, no, please, not the martini.

It will be an outdoor cafe, when the weather changes. For now, the external area is encased in heavy plastic. We are inside, catching up on family news and reminiscing. The days that she spent in my apartment, our three-year-old daughters hugging, seem all so long ago. She says she has changed, is no longer insecure. She now speaks up for herself. We share a rigid

German upbringing. We laugh, dredging up German expressions learned from our parents. I am not sure that I have changed all that much. We are still, respectively, 22 and 29 years old, at a tacky little bar in New York.

98. AVATAR

I don't want to write about my history of hiding during the war or of immigration and eventual integration into a new world. Yet, whenever I start putting words on paper, I end up exploring my abandonment issues. Too much psychoanalysis! Plunging into anecdotes of my dance world proved a tonic. Now, I have run dry, need new experiences, a new persona.

I heard a talk on the radio about creating avatars and living a virtual life. Avatars meet up, fall in love, get married and presumably get divorced too. I don't understand any of this. I am the wrong generation. Do you get married when your avatar does? What if you're married already? I can understand having different selves, but they can't really live separate lives in the world. My more adventurous self can't climb Mount Everest without taking me along and I don't want to go.

Is this all a way of escaping complexity, of creating one-dimensional selves.? When you work in therapy, with people who have Multiple Personality Disorders, their alters represent different parts of themselves. None of them struggle with ambivalence and none is a complete person. One is good at solving problems, one is seductive, one has the role of protecting the system with fierce, often misplaced aggression. So, what are avatars? I fear there is no way of avoiding angst and misery, even in this "brave new world".

But they say, everyone has a double. I discovered mine on the occasion of my tango performance with Emil.

There's an announcement that there is to be a Tango Open House, with a free group lesson at which I am to do a demonstration or "show," with Emil. On the appointed day, when I arrive toting three bottles of wine, as promised, there are two couples taking the lesson, my entire audience.

Though my friends don't normally come, there are usually more students. Emil tells me that ten people promised to come but, "You can lead a horse to water, etc...." On the whole, I am relieved. He says that I look gorgeous, but then one takes such statements with a grain of salt. I am still nervous, and my feet hurt in my heels. Is it a particularly ungiving floor? Also, it's cold in the studio. Emil looks at me expectantly and says: "Should we wait? Is anyone else coming?" "No," I say. "Let's do it." I think: "Let's get it over with."

There are some "oohs and ahs" at the lifts and twirls. These are beginners and they tell me how amazing I am. This too mustn't be taken too seriously, though it's tempting to believe. One woman agrees to tape the four-minute dance on my iPad. When I check later there is nothing. It's a non-event.

But it is the conversation afterwards that stays with me. A curly-headed full-bodied woman approaches me. She, too, apparently dances with Miguel. She declares, "He's special. What a heart he has!" She tells me that she escaped from Ukraine in the 90s with her 11-year-old daughter. She was alone but she managed to become a nurse and she works a second job to afford the dance lessons. She tells me about her successful daughter, a psychiatrist, I think. The daughter went to the Bronx High School of Science and then to Brandeis University. What does it mean that I too came to this country at eleven years old and went to Bronx Science and to Brandeis, am in the Mental Health profession, and that she and I do tango with Miguel? Undoubtedly, it's a mere coincidence. Would I like her daughter who, in some way, walks in my footsteps? Was my spending all these hours going down to Manhattan, learning this dance, leading me towards talking to this woman? I want to know more of my other self.

When I get home, take off my dress and wash my face, I reflect that anyway it is sort of brave to agree to perform and to follow through, in spite of my misgivings. It wasn't a bad choreography and Emil seemed genuinely pleased. And there is some other version of me somewhere in New York.

99. HOPE

If you were to ask me what impels me to drive downtown, through heavy traffic in any kind of weather to dance, I might tell you about seeing the 99-year-old poet, Stanley Kunitz, reciting these lines from one of his poems: "what makes the engine go? / Desire, desire, desire."

For many years, I have been anticipating the end of my mobility. Any twinge of pain sounds the alarm. Illness, surgery could stop my dancing. Of course, old age, the mounting of the years has been my reality for a long time. But watching the documentary, *Capturing Grace,* through a mist of tears inspires me, gives me hope. It occurs to me that maybe it is possible to dance, in some fashion, if you want to, until the day you die, even if that means just moving your hand or just imagining moving effortlessly through space.

The film documents the experience of an unusually brave group of dancers. They all struggle against the constraints of Parkinson's Disease. Some of them have been trapped inside the extreme limitations of their bodies for as much as twenty years. Some of these people cannot walk easily or tie their shoes or open a door due to the rigidity of their limbs or because of incapacitating tremors. Nevertheless, according to the director of the film and to their teacher, principal dancer of the Mark Morris Company, "They are not patients, they are dancers This is not therapy, it is art." The director of the film, who himself was given the dread diagnosis, says that, "They all lost something, but the dream of moving freely persists." Some come in walkers or in wheelchairs. None of them can do a perfect turn or point their toes, or even stand erect. It is the struggle to move beyond the constraints of their bodies, not the virtuosity of the movement that gives the dance its poignancy. When the woman sitting on a chair opens up her arms and smiles, she is for now free, moving in space, flying perhaps. She cannot walk, but she can dance when the music leads her into another realm from that of ordinary life. The woman, moving through her violent spasms, is transcending fear and self-doubt and in the process telling a story with her body. For that moment she is not anticipating her further decline; she isn't thinking about the possibility that her medication will no longer work in another week, another month. She is dancing.

They dance as a group, connecting with each other, sending a blessing to the next person in the circle. Everyone comes to rehearsal every day, sick, afraid, or in pain, in spite of everything. There will be a show and they are a Dance Company, even though they don't look like traditional dancers. Their teacher, David Leventhal, says, "The common idea is that there are dancers and everyone else. I think that's a tragedy." He asserts that teaching this group is no different from teaching a class of professionals. It is the struggle to learn to stretch just a little further that makes the dance meaningful. I find myself not interested in the professionals but moved by the expressiveness of the new dancers, who meet this unexpected challenge with trepidation and joy.

Alexey's words about doing your "personal best' resonate with a deeper meaning for me now. You do not have to have Lila's extensions, Dora's sharp technique. You will never dance like Natalya, but you can reach higher, get closer to bringing the dance to life, to learning to be fully present in the moment in each movement.

100. FACING THE REAL WORLD

Emily Dickinson wrote, "Not knowing when dawn will come/I open every door". I say, not knowing when the end will come, I open every door. I want to say, "yes and yes and yes." But it feels so easy to stay entrapped in lifelong patterns of hiding.

Every few decades, I pledge to be more engaged with the outside world, but I retreat. I can't bear the brutality of the real world. I am ever more thin-skinned, as I know that war and torture are ubiquitous, that few are spared. I read a lot, mostly novels that offer redemption through their beauty and the hope that there is love, in spite of tragedy and loss.

So, shall I open myself now to the supernatural? In theory, it is less messy, no blood, no third-degree burns, or so I think. My fantasy is of messages from another world in the form of sudden warmth, glittering lights, unknown sweet melodies. But what of paralyzing cold, explosions, oozing ectoplasm. I think of Shirley Jackson's brilliant novel, *The Haunting of Hill House*, full of portents that lead to terror and death. I want my supernatural domesticated, free of tooth and claw.

I don't change much, in spite of resolutions. I crave warmth and beauty, the way a plant needs water. I flinch at loud noises. I admire photojournalists who travel into war zones, but I don't have the fortitude to face even a minuscule fraction of the human misery they record.

In this, the last part of my life, I must acknowledge that I will have lived and will die a coward, so someone who "cowers." On the other hand, there may be something to be said for embracing the people you know, thrilling to the beauty of words, music, the budding trees in your back yard. Voltaire's creation, Candide declares, after experiencing the cruelty of the world, "We must cultivate our garden." I have come full circle. It is acceptable, perhaps, to just be myself. And I will dance to defeat the demons.